Praise for
THE **PLAN**

"Ladies, this is the book we've been waiting for. *The PLAN* is a time-management book written by a woman with women in mind. It's practical, funny, and is changing the way we see lists and organizing our lives. We loved every mention of our uterine walls shedding. And there's a Matrix reference. Kendra Adachi understands. She's here for you."

> —JENNA FISCHER AND ANGELA KINSEY, hosts of the
> *Office Ladies* podcast

"Kendra Adachi is the go-to for smart, pragmatic, knowing analysis of time and tasks. I turn to her to keep me oriented toward what matters. She's a gift."

> —KELLY CORRIGAN, *New York Times* bestselling author
> and host of the *Kelly Corrigan Wonders* podcast

"Strikingly original and compassionate, Kendra Adachi offers a vision of time management that embraces the unique messiness of your life instead of trying to optimize it away."

> —CAL NEWPORT, *New York Times* bestselling author of
> *Slow Productivity* and *Digital Minimalism*

"Are you a human? Then you are going to love this book . . . tender, compassionate, infinitely useful. You'll walk away a little more convinced that some plans are worth it and others were programmed into you in the 2000s during low-fat yogurt commercials about women having it all."

> —KATE BOWLER, *New York Times* bestselling author of
> *Everything Happens for a Reason*

"After delving into countless time-management books, *The PLAN* emerges as the awaited gem. A vital voice in time management, Kendra Adachi skillfully normalizes the challenges specific to women and equips us with practical tools for success. This overdue perspective is a breath of fresh air."

—NEDRA GLOVER TAWWAB, *New York Times* bestselling author of *Set Boundaries, Find Peace*

"Kendra Adachi is a generous teacher with a refreshing framework for how to plan your life like a person, not a robot. Smart, wise, and right on time, this is the most accessible time-management book I've ever read."

—EMILY P. FREEMAN, *New York Times* bestselling author of *How to Walk into a Room*

"If I had to choose only one book as a guide for the remainder of my journey toward wholeness, it would be this one! The brilliance of Kendra Adachi is demonstrated in her unsurpassed ability to name the differences between men and women while respecting both. For women who are making our way in the twenty-first century, she asks all the right questions and offers solutions that work, while proving that equality does not mean sameness. I've needed this book since I was nineteen years old, yet at seventy-three it's not too late!"

—SUZANNE STABILE, co-author of *The Road Back to You,* author of *The Path Between Us,* and host of *The Enneagram Journey* podcast

"*The PLAN* is for readers who have hormones, bosses, and homes to manage (hopefully with an equal partner), who have found the current time-management tools lacking."

—EVE RODSKY, *New York Times* bestselling author of *Fair Play*

THE
PLAN

THE
PLAN

Manage Your Time Like a Lazy Genius

Kendra Adachi

CONVERGENT
NEW YORK

Published in the United States by Convergent Books, an imprint of Random House, a division of Penguin Random House LLC, New York.

CONVERGENT BOOKS is a registered trademark and the Convergent colophon is a trademark of Penguin Random House LLC.

Kendra Joyner Adachi is represented by Alive Literary Agency, www.aliveliterary.com.

Hardback ISBN 978-0-593-72793-5
Ebook ISBN 978-0-593-72794-2

Printed in the United States of America on acid-free paper

convergentbooks.com

9 8 7 6 5 4 3 2 1

First Edition

Illustrations and hand lettering by Sarah Horgan
Book design by Ralph Fowler

For the Neighbors:

Your enthusiasm for this book

made me want to keep going.

Thank you for cheering me on.

Contents

Part Three: **Pep Talks**

Author's Note

I wrote this book to help you in any life stage.

Whether you are partnered, single, a parent, a student, working, retired, or literally anything else, you can use this refreshingly helpful, mildly subversive framework to manage your time.

That said, your life is full of specific challenges that cannot fit within the pages of this one book. If you'd like help with a particular area of life that *The PLAN* doesn't cover, check out *The Lazy Genius Podcast.* There you'll find hundreds of episodes on a variety of topics that will likely offer what you need.

I'm grateful you're here.

Yes, We *Do* Need Another Time-Management Book

I have a long history of being meticulous.

As a kid, I enjoyed folding laundry into beautiful piles, vacuuming to get those breathtaking carpet lines, and shelving my Nancy Drew books by publication date. I knew how to make my bed with hospital corners as a third grader *because I asked my mom to show me how.*

As a teenager, I got even cooler. I had an impeccable work ethic, a perpetually clean room, and a stack of notebooks that held my future goals, my favorite movies, and, inexplicably, my classmates' names in alphabetical order. By first *and* last name. I still don't understand why.

You might think that as a grown woman I would've relaxed a little, but you would be wrong. I had a color-coded binder of every helpful *Real Simple* article ever published, an annual cleaning schedule on my fridge (yes, I said *annual*), and enough five-year plans to fill a dozen lifetimes. And please don't ask me to count how many planners I've purchased in my twentyish years of adulthood. The answer is likely in the triple digits, and our relationship needs more time before I'm that vulnerable.

In short, I love it when my life is in order.

However, in my early thirties, after bringing three kids and two side hustles into the world, I was bone tired from just living my life, and I could not figure out why. I had done the right things! I had read dozens of the most popular self-help books and organized my life according to their principles, but all that did was make me a caffeinated squirrel on a treadmill.

I thought the problem was me. Maybe I didn't have enough discipline or consistency. Maybe I had misidentified my goals and therefore couldn't make them happen. Maybe I needed a new _planner._

Bless.

Because I consistently experienced a disconnect between popular self-help strategies and my actual life, I felt I needed to bridge the gap, but I couldn't figure out how.

That's why I wrote my first book, _The Lazy Genius Way._ It's a collection of thirteen principles that you can apply to any problem in any season of life.* It's a personal, versatile approach to living a good life based on what matters to you, instead of choosing a life because someone else said it was good. In fact, _The Lazy Genius Way_ felt so comprehensive to me that I thought it would be my only book.

Again, bless.

My second book, _The Lazy Genius Kitchen,_ applied those same thirteen Lazy Genius principles to the kitchen, and right after its release, I was confident _that_ was my last book. What else could I possibly say?

This, apparently.

The initial idea for _The PLAN_ did not come from anything interesting, like a lightbulb moment in the shower or an idea written on a cocktail napkin in the darkened bowels of a dive bar. Nope. It came from data analysis. Riveting.

I run a content-creation business, and it's important for my

---

*You can find them in the Quick-Reference Guide at the end of the book.

team and me to know what content resonates so we can know what to create. The data says that the most popular episodes of _The Lazy Genius Podcast_ are, by a significant margin, all related to time management. Annual survey responses say the same: "Kendra, you can stop talking about the other stuff; just talk to us about how to not drown in our to-do lists!"

And frankly, I'm good at it. At my core, I'm still the third grader who loves hospital corners and alphabetized lists, but I'm also an adult who's had enough therapy, failure, and rewarding relationships to put my love of order in a healthy context. As a result, I enjoy speaking about refreshing and occasionally subversive ways to manage our time so we can just _live our lives._

But as I flirted with what this book could be, I noticed something that changed everything—I am a woman.

I mean, I knew that already, but in the context of time-management books? There aren't a lot of us. In fact, 93 percent of time-management books are written by men. Ninety-actual-three.*

Guess what that means?

The problem isn't you.

It's not your lack of dedication, consistency, or motivation. It's not because you haven't started the right habit or taken the right online course. It's because the current productivity paradigm doesn't work for women. It's that simple. The advice you're getting is for men by men, and women are just expected to make it work.

Think about it. Most time-management authors and experts are men who do not have a boss, a home to run, or a menstrual cycle. I don't know if you're aware, but all three are notoriously

---

*I did my own analysis of the top-selling books over several decades, recommended reading lists, and what is on store shelves. Whether the sample size was seventeen or seventeen hundred, the number written by men was always 93 percent. Wild.

unwieldy. And if you're not wielding them on a regular basis, it's much easier to create your ideal life.

> # The current productivity paradigm doesn't work for women.

If you don't have a boss, you can craft a work schedule where you check email twice a day and go home at 3 P.M. If you're not managing meals, moods, and the entire family calendar, you can prioritize your health, friendships, and leisure. If you're un-affected by weekly hormonal fluctuations, you can create an ideal day and replicate it.

In general, a man's life is oriented around *him,* and a woman's life is oriented around everything *but her,* all while her body's rhythms are annoyingly inconvenient.

This exclusion is why most productivity books are incomplete. They were written by and for a certain subset, and you are likely not in that subset. You will struggle to follow their rules because you're not meant to play their game.

Of course, there's nothing wrong with a man's system and the authors who keep it standing. I'm glad they have approaches that work for their particular lives, but they don't comprehensively work for ours. The current productivity landscape misses us—women and anyone else who lives outside the traditional white-male experience—and I'm tired of so many people being missed.

For the record, this book is not anti–white guy. I love white guys. (I'd say I'm married to one, but that would be a lie since my husband, Kaz, is Japanese.) Some of my favorite books are written by white guys. Some of my favorite friends are white guys. I'm not knocking them in general or in the context of productivity.

I simply want to acknowledge that the current time-management paradigm is *not for us.* The loudest voices are not our voices, and their strategies are not what we need.

And that is why we *do* need another time-management book.

How to Read This Book

I've divided *The PLAN* into three sections: principles, strategies, and pep talks. I tried to make them all start with a *p,* but it was a lost cause.

Part 1 teaches the **principles** of *The PLAN*. Since belief comes before behavior, you need to understand *why* before you learn *how.*

Part 2 is that *how.* In it, I'll teach you **strategies** for managing your time that are practical, tangible, and without an ounce of bootstrap energy.

Part 3 is an entire section of **pep talks**. Each one is specific to a particular time-management struggle, and they are not meant to be read all at once. Instead, when you feel off-kilter, skim the pep talk titles, read one that resonates, and then get back to your life with your feet a little firmer on the ground.

The PLAN is full of lists, steps, and frameworks (all drenched in humanity and compassion, I promise), and you might want to remember something without skimming the entire book to find it. In those instances, go straight to the Quick-Reference Guide.

The PLAN is intended to be your time-management companion from this day forward. Write in it. Dog-ear pages. Use one highlighter color for your personal life and another color for your work life. Keep *The PLAN* with your planner. Regularly read a pep talk. Revisit the principles when you feel overwhelmed by your life. Try a new strategy during a new season.

Every reading will illuminate something new.

I'm grateful to be here with you, honored by your trust, and hopeful you will reach for this book often.

Let's get started.

Part One
Principles

Consider the next few chapters your entrance to Oz. The transformative principles of *The PLAN* will take you from the black-and-white binary of the self-help industry to the Technicolor dreamland of being a Lazy Genius. I can't wait for this section to help you see your time in a brand-new way.

Now, there's a chance you think you already know what I'm going to say. If you're familiar with either me or self-help books in general, you might make assumptions about these principles— thinking that you know them, are fine without them, and can just skip to the strategies. I've done that myself when reading books like this. When you're well versed in the language of productivity, principles are just the page fillers before you get to the good stuff.

Except when it comes to *The PLAN*.

These principles will surprise you. In fact, writing this book felt like opening Mary Poppins's carpetbag—every time I reached inside, I pulled out something else magical that I didn't know was there. *The PLAN*'s principles will go down differently. I promise.

We desperately need a new approach for managing our time, and that begins with a new way to *see*. *The PLAN* is your lens.

1. **The Real Reason Planning Is Hard**

I grew up going to the mall.

If you're of an age where you're not sure what a mall is, now is a good time to tell you that I'm in perimenopause, I've never downloaded TikTok, and I didn't have a cellphone until I was seventeen. Not because my parents were strict but because *people didn't have them yet.* Consider yourself generationally warned.

Back to the mall. I loved spending time there as a kid. The mall is where I got my ears pierced, where I awkwardly hung out with a boy I liked, where I ate a truckload of Cinnabons, and where I learned to confidently walk past Victoria's Secret without looking or breaking stride.*

But my favorite thing about the mall was the "You Are Here" map. Holy moly, I *still* love that thing. Not only do you have the stores organized by category on a giant screen, but you also have a beautiful red dot that tells you exactly where you are.**

---

*Say you grew up in purity culture without saying you grew up in purity culture.

**Say you're an Enneagram 1 without saying you're an Enneagram 1.

You can see everything, *and* you can see yourself.

Chances are you'd like that for your life, too. Wouldn't it be *amazing* to see everything at a glance so you can quickly chart a route to an imagined future where life is beautiful and under control?

That's probably why you keep buying planners.

A planner is the closest thing we have to a "You Are Here" map, to that bird's-eye view. You want your day, week, month, quarter, year, to-do lists, tracking bubbles, words of gratitude, meal plans, and five-year goals all available at a glance.

You get your next new planner and spend hours setting it up, answering questions about what you want to accomplish and what habits you want to begin, and maybe even trying your hand at a doodle or two. Once you're done, you let out a deep, gratified sigh. *There it is! There's everything at once! Life is going to be better now!*

But then, much to your chagrin, life happens again, and you can't keep up with your plan. You manage what you can for as long as you can, biding your time until the next opportunity to reset and see everything at once—the beginning of summer, the school year, January—and you repeat.

I bet you've been repeating for a long time, yet you're still drowning. Why?

"Everything at once" is the *problem, not the solution.*

> # "Everything at once" is the *problem, not the solution.*

"Everything at once" is why you push your palms against your eyeballs multiple times a day. "Everything at once" is why you doomscroll in the bathroom, hoping no one notices you're gone. (They will.) "Everything at once" is why you listen to an audiobook while cooking dinner while helping somebody with homework while wearing microfiber socks because somebody on the internet said it was like sweeping.

"Everything at once" is not how we're meant to live.

Before you lose hope, let me be the Robin Williams to your Matt Damon and tell you that it's not your fault. It's not your fault. *It's not your fault.**

You are not the reason you're drowning. *You* are not the reason "everything at once" doesn't work. *You* are not the reason time-management principles aren't sticking.

The reason is far beyond you.

The System Is Rigged

Let's sit crisscross-applesauce and do a little History Corner.

Remember the Industrial Revolution? America quickly went from "Whoa, coal!" to "OMG, gas is amazing!" to "Have you heard about this electricity thing?" The West got bigger and better and, consequently, went cuckoo for productivity. This guy's factory had to beat that guy's factory, and he did that by making stuff faster than the other guy did.

When the digital revolution happened, it gave us more than computers and AOL Instant Messenger. We were given the promise of more *time.* Technology would create efficient production *for* us, freeing us to do other, presumably more enjoyable, things. Amazing!

However, that digital revolution happened so fast that we never disentangled ourselves from the Industrial Revolution's culture of productivity. Unfortunately for us, that same technology incidentally made the productivity obsession worse.

---

*Please tell me you've seen *Good Will Hunting.*

It makes me think of that scene in *Sabrina* when Harrison Ford (Linus) and Julia Ormond (Sabrina) take a helicopter to board a private jet to fly to Martha's Vineyard for the day. Once they're buckled into their plush seats, Linus immediately begins working, looking at nothing but the reports in front of him.

Sabrina, frustrated by his indifference to the present moment, asks, "Don't you ever look out the window?"

"I don't have time."

"What about all that time we saved taking the helicopter?"

He awkwardly pauses. "I'm storing it up."

"No, you're not," she replies.[1]

And we're not either.

In fact, the obsession with productivity is so deeply woven into our culture that we live in a **productivity-industrial complex.** Even though I did not thrive in any form of social studies class, allow me to explain what that means.

An industrial complex is essentially when an industry is in a feedback loop with some element in society. The public and private sectors become so intertwined that separating them is almost impossible, and that connection is often at odds with what's best for society itself.

Let's take weddings as an example. The U.S. wedding industry was worth over $70 billion in 2023, with the average wedding costing just shy of thirty grand.[2] I'm not knocking anyone's choices, and if you want an all-out wedding, enjoy it. But what if the wedding industry began pushing the idea that smaller, simpler, less expensive weddings were great, that you didn't need to follow the trends, think about Instagram-worthy elements, or be impressive in any way? If that idea took root, people would spend less, and the industry would suffer. So even though it might be collectively better for folks to have whatever wedding they like, *the wedding industry cannot encourage that.* Therefore, we will continue to have magazines, blogs, and social media telling us what kind of wedding we *should* want. That's a wedding-industrial complex.

Another example is the prison-industrial complex. Many are championing reform in the judicial system, which would lead to fewer people in prisons. However, the U.S. prison industry makes more than $10 billion a year, and incarcerated individuals in the prison system generate revenue from goods and services on top of that.[3] So even though justice reform and prison reform would be beneficial for society, the prison-industrial complex makes them extremely difficult because of how deeply entwined the justice system is with industry.

The same has happened with productivity.

This Is a Man's World

The current productivity paradigm of optimization, efficiency, and success is so pervasive and so *expected* that it stands to reason we need resources and structures to uphold that paradigm. The global productivity industry is projected to generate $79 *billion* in 2024.[4] That's a lot of billions.

As long as productivity matters, the marketplace will thrive, and as long as the marketplace thrives, productivity will remain in the cultural conversation. The snake just eats its tail while also becoming very rich.

And that snake does not want you to be content with your life. That snake wants you to keep trying and striving and planning and dreaming and wondering if any of it is working. That snake wants you to, as the horrible saying goes, *rest when you're dead,* because when *you* keep going, you spend money and keep the industry going, too. As my friend and *New York Times* bestselling author Kelly Corrigan once said to me, "Contentment doesn't stimulate economic activity."

In short, your preoccupation with productivity, to whatever level, is not your fault. It was built into the system long before you were flipping through your first planner. And that's not the only thing that's built into the system.

Now it's time for *Women's* History Corner . . .

White women couldn't vote until 1920.

Black women couldn't vote until 1965.*

Women could legally be fired for being pregnant until 1978.

Women still get paid less than men for the same jobs.

Oh, fun! We can throw a little implicit patriarchy into the productivity-industrial complex!

Essentially, women are in a white-man-made world that's supported by white men's rules for the benefit of white men, and we haven't had a voice for long enough to see many tangible results of being heard.

Exceptions exist everywhere, but generally speaking, men aren't expected to make every meal, do all the laundry, remember every birthday, "get their body back," stay at home for the sake of the kids, or have kids at all. They're not shamed for being single. They don't worry about going for a run at night or automatically walk through a parking deck with their keys between their fingers. Men don't daily exist with the weariness and injustice of not being listened to in a male-dominated field. They aren't the ones to leave work to get a sick kid from school. Men typically do not take it upon themselves to remember every detail of a home's invisible ecosystem. Men aren't told to smile, calm down, clean up, or get in line. Men don't bleed every twenty-eight days.

Do you see the disparity here? The productivity industry makes a ton of money teaching us to produce, all within a culture that holds us to a startlingly high standard of what a woman's production should be. We have no choice but to live according to the rules and strategies written by and for men.

It's exhausting, and it's time for another way.

---

*After the Civil War, many Southern states adopted discriminatory voting practices, which the Voting Rights Act of 1965 outlawed.

TO RECAP

Plain and simple, our cultural systems, including the current system of productivity, were not built for women. We live in a productivity-industrial complex built on male-dominated systems and strategies, which does not have our best interests in mind. But since that system is all women have, we think *we're* the problem when it doesn't work, and we just keep trying harder.

The system doesn't need tweaking—the system is broken.

It's time for a whole new paradigm.

2. **Two Beliefs That Will Change Everything**

According to internet memes, Hall of Fame football coach Lou Holtz once said, "If you're bored with life, if you don't get up every morning with a burning desire to do things, you don't have enough goals."

Listen, I can't remember the last time I woke up with a burning desire to do anything except maybe go back to sleep.

We've already established that if you dig until you hit bottom, you'll find a productivity-industrial complex fueled by patriarchy. Fun times. The flowers growing out of that gnarly soil include possibility, potential, striving, and optimization:

"Shoot your shot."

"Reach for the stars."

"Don't squander your potential."

"Imagine the life you want, and don't stop until you get there."

"Be great."

I'm already tired.

Allow me to introduce you to the first belief that changes everything: **The goal is not greatness.**

The goal is not mastery over your habits or power over your day. It's not creating an ideal schedule and then duplicating it until you're dead. We're also not here to "crush" anything. The word alone gives me a headache.

But if the goal is not greatness, then what is it?

It's integration.

Greatness vs. Integration

Integration is a word used in various psychological contexts and essentially means "wholeness." When we are integrated, we are able to connect with all the parts of ourselves—desires, bodily cues, big emotions that we don't know what to do with, small emotions that don't feel important, stress responses when things go awry, grief that sneaks up on us, anger because we stepped on a Lego, and literally everything that happens moment by moment. When we are integrated, we compassionately love our true selves and seek to live smack-dab in the center of who we know ourselves to be.

Renowned vulnerability researcher and *New York Times* bestselling author Brené Brown describes integration as "whole-hearted living" and suggests letting go of these ten things in order to live wholeheartedly:

1. What people think

2. Perfectionism

3. Numbing and powerlessness

4. Scarcity and fear of the dark

5. Need for certainty

6. Comparison

7. Exhaustion as a status symbol or productivity as self-worth

8. Anxiety as a lifestyle

9. Self-doubt and "supposed to"

10. Cool and always in control[1]

The more we let these ten things fall away, the more integrated we become.

> # When we are integrated, we compassionately love our true selves and seek to live smack-dab in the center of who we know ourselves to be.

Here's another way to look at it. Therapist and author Aundi Kolber describes integration as bringing parts back to the whole, like "a magnet pulling these elements of yourself back in with compassion and care."[2]

Consider these phrases she offers regarding integration:

I can stay with myself.

I can be gentle with myself.

I am beloved.

It's okay to be in process.

I am making progress.

I can come back to myself.

I am responsible for only myself.

It's okay for others to be uncomfortable.

I am allowed to take care of myself.[3]

Now look at these two lists—Brown's guideposts for whole-heartedness and Kolber's phrases for integration—and pay attention to what's happening in your body.

Maybe your breathing has slowed or you just experienced a deep sigh. Your shoulders might relax. You suddenly feel a sweet pull of permission to let something go.

Next, I'm going to share another list. These are the eight principles required to achieve greatness from a male author's bestselling productivity book:

1. Create a vision.

2. Turn adversity into advantage.

3. Cultivate a champion's mindset.

4. Develop hustle.

5. Master your body.

6. Practice positive habits.

7. Build a winning team.

8. Be of service to others.[4]

These are not bad statements. Some are great and might deeply resonate with you. There's no judgment here. But notice how your body feels after reading that list, especially compared with the other two. The energy in *my* body definitely shifts. I go from a relaxed state to a more elevated one. I take a deep breath but for a different reason. I don't want to be great or master mastery or hustle my way to that patriarchal paradigm of what a good life looks like and how to get it. It's just not for me.

And not to be a downer, but women don't get the same opportunities to practice these principles of greatness anyway. I'd like to see a man master a body that regularly and painfully releases uterine lining and might occasionally birth a human baby.

I don't want to master my body. I want to tend to it.

I say this in my work all the time because we constantly need to hear it: *You're not a robot.* You're not a machine to program. You're not a steadily humming operating system. You're not something to fix, leverage, or optimize.

You're a flesh-and-blood person with a beautiful, slightly unruly life who just wants to get your stuff done, have fun, not yell at your people too much, and occasionally feel bone-deep contentment. You want to make hard things a little easier and enjoy life more often than you endure it.

> # You want to make hard things a little easier and enjoy life more often than you endure it.

You want to continue becoming more deeply and confidently yourself.

The goal can't be greatness, not for people who are trying to live wholeheartedly. Instead, **we seek integration.**

Quick side note: Can you garner greatness, favor, even fame, and still be integrated? Yep. But if your goal is greatness, if that's the most important thing, you're going in the wrong order, at least for the kind of life I think you want to live.

The goal is not greatness. The goal is integration.

Start Where You Are

Here's the second belief that changes everything: **Start where you are.**

Most time-management tools start with where you want to go. Each book, course, and planner is an open invitation to a shiny new "You Are Here" map. The typical order is to think about your life; imagine how you want it to look in five, ten, twenty years; consider multiple categories like health, finances, relationships, and career fulfillment; and break your broader hopes for those categories into manageable goals that you'll spread across the coming days. Congratulations! Now you know how to organize and maximize your life, and you'll accomplish your dreams in no time.

While that approach might work for some, it has never worked for me.

I'm a lady with a cantankerous menstrual cycle, a gaggle of children who could not be more different in how they need their mother, a business that partially depends on the whims of the internet and whatever creativity I can muster on any given day, and a million other things I can't even name because I'm too overstimulated.

There is no tool complex enough to hold the intricacies and daily variability of a woman's life, even though I've spent hours trying to make one. You probably have, too. But remember, we are not the problem. A patriarchal society that birthed a productivity-industrial complex that keeps selling us tools that ignore our needs and lived experience is the problem.

> # There is no tool complex enough to hold the intricacies and daily variability of a woman's life.

We don't start with where we want to go.
We start where we already are.
Is where you're going important? Totally. This is not an all-or-nothing argument. Just like you can be integrated and achieve greatness, you can also be present and plan for the future.
But first, we need to tend to ourselves today. Right now.
This season. This body. This family. This crisis. This financial situation. This transition. This holiday. This school project. This

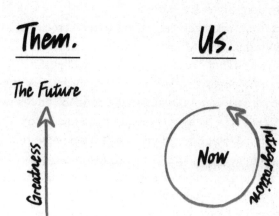

Them.

Us.

The Future

Greatness

Now

Integration

work deadline. This tantrum. This headache. This meal. This walk. This deep breath. *This moment.*

I have a more accurate and even joyful perspective about my future *when I stay rooted in my present,* and I think the same can be true for you. As you slowly incorporate the strategies and mindsets in this book, you will have a greater sense of compassion and—dare I say—accomplishment *today,* and the more often you experience days like that, the more your future aligns with who you most deeply are.

Don't assume that pursuing greatness based on an invisible future is your only option. You can, instead, seek integration right where you are today.

Embrace Your Taco Floatie

So far, I've told you that the system is broken *and* that your pursuit of capturing "everything at once" is not the solution you think it is. I promise I won't always be a downer. But it's vital that you recognize the danger of "everything at once" and know how to navigate the feeling when it comes. My therapist helped me visualize that process, and since it was helpful for me, maybe it will be for you, too.

When I am living from "everything at once" on my "You Are Here" map, I feel like I'm drowning in the ocean, and I assume the only way to *not drown* is to get to the shore.

But I can't teleport. I can't immediately go from the middle of the deepest water straight to the beach. Regular life doesn't work that way.

What I can do is breathe and slowly find my way to the floatie close by. Choose your preferred shape, but mine is a taco. I grab on, catch my breath, and wait a minute. After some rest, I might have the strength to kick a little to reach the floating platform between me and the shore. There's no rush, though. I'm present with my taco floatie. Eventually, I gather enough calming strength within myself to get to the beach. First, I sit in the shallow surf. Maybe for a while. Then at some point, with a stretch of my creaky knees, I stand with two feet on the ground.

Learning to be present and kind to yourself, no matter where you are in the water, doesn't happen all at once. It's slow work. But it's a process you can trust.

Being a person is not an exercise in optimization, in drafting a comprehensive plan and then pressing a red Start button. That is not the life we want. I'm not saying *don't* plan ahead or invest for retirement or set goals. Those things all count, especially if you want them to.

> **Being a person is not an exercise in optimization, in drafting a comprehensive plan and then pressing a red Start button. That is not the life we want.**

But starting from there? Especially when you're definitely in the deepest water just trying to get through today? That's not being kind to yourself. And if you're a woman, it's a lost cause anyway. The pressure on women is so heavy, so obtuse, and so unreasonable that we cannot compassionately expect ourselves to start with the future, not effectively anyway, even though we've done an excellent job trying.

It's time for something different.

TO RECAP

We need a break from the current time-management paradigm because its goal is different from ours. Its goal is greatness, mastery, and power over as many details as possible. Ours is to be wholehearted and integrated, starting where we are.

Now it's time to learn how.

3. Begin with What Matters to You

The primary reason standard productivity approaches leave us wanting is that they see life as one big task, one big objective, one big system to get us across a finish line. You're supposed to name what you want out of life, what you hope to achieve, and what dreams you want to pursue in the giant, singular future with little to no thought of the season you're in now.

Since our goal is integration and we start where we are, *what matters right now in this season* is the most important thing we can initially consider and will positively influence the rest of your life.

Think for a moment about all the different seasons you've been in: moving to a new city, adjusting to having a kid or two or five, being single for the first time in your adult life, being in the middle of a renovation, looking for a job, waiting for a diagnosis, walking with someone else through their own illness. Do you live the exact same way during all those seasons? I hope not! Your needs and your perception of those needs change with your circumstances and even as you age, so making different choices about how you live and spend your time is natural and wise.

Naming what matters is aligning your needs with your season, no matter what is happening. You are paying attention to *right now,* honoring the life that is in front of you. And the more you practice asking, the more natural naming will become.

> # Naming what matters is aligning your needs with your season, no matter what is happening.

But how do you know the answer? How do you know what matters most right where you are?

When you ask what matters, you are likely asking in one of two postures: **proactive** or **reactive.** Let's learn about both.

Proactively naming what matters is when you consider what you know to be coming: a new job, a pregnancy, a move to a new neighborhood or city, summer break, a huge work project. You know you're about to enter a new season or situation and want to prepare for it well.

Reactively naming what matters is when you consider the unexpected or unplanned: your boss asking you to stay late at work, your period starting early, your carpool arrangement falling through, your train running late, your kid needing to poop just as you're walking out the door. This requires a much quicker turnaround and is occasionally followed by just a smidge of stress eating.

In the process of naming what matters, the first step is to know if you are asking proactively or reactively. That answer is thankfully quite clear.

Now the two roads diverge a little. Let's first walk down the path of *proactively* naming what matters.

Proactively Naming What Matters

The fact that you're proactively trying to figure out what matters is already worth a celebration. You're looking ahead but in a very present way. You're not asking what matters about your entire life, focusing on the distant future and hoping to command a certain level of control over time itself. You're simply paying attention to where you are and hoping to figure out what matters in this next season. Way to go.

But how do you actually know? It's simple: **Make what matters singular, then make it smaller.** Let's dive into what that means.

Life transitions feel big and overwhelming because they're multifaceted. It's challenging to proactively name what matters about a looming new thing like a kid or job or breakup when the transition affects so many aspects of life. How are you supposed to tend to everything at once? Frankly, you can't. Instead, choose one aspect that matters most right now. In other words, make it singular.

Start by asking what could matter about this life transition. Write down all the things that feel important. If you're starting a new work project that involves a lot more traveling and late nights, the things that could matter are maintaining connections with family and friends, tending to your tired body, finding energy to stay focused and creative during the project, delegating tasks that you usually do to someone else, and making sure you're getting enough sleep.

Now that you have these possibilities and see them all in front of you, what stands out? What actually *does* matter to you? Let's say it's staying connected to your family and getting enough sleep. Great. When confronted with situations throughout the day, you know to prioritize those two things.

But what happens on the nights when you get home at nine instead of six? In that moment, do you choose family or sleep?

When your priorities are at odds with each other, it's common to waffle between the two for so long that you lose your chance at either, and that's not our ideal scenario here. Instead, decide what matters *most.* You might not need to make that choice very often, but it's helpful to know what to choose when you're stuck between two things that matter.

> # When your priorities are at odds with each other, it's common to waffle between the two for so long that you lose your chance at either.

Let's go back to the work project idea. You might be the type of person who is an absolute terror on too little sleep, and that lack of sleep affects everything else that matters. You can't be present with your family because you're tired. You don't have the energy to stay creative and focused on the project because you're tired. You don't have patience or flexibility in the airport when you're traveling because you're tired. You can't go for a mental health run because you're tired. If that's the case, sleep is your singular priority. Now when you're wondering whether to get up with the kids on Saturday morning or leave that to your partner so you can sleep in, you choose sleeping in. Sleep is your singular priority in this season, and that knowledge helps you manage your energy and make decisions with more thoughtfulness. Plus, have you ever tried to play pretend with a kid while groggy? You're not a good time. Get your sleep. It makes everything, including playing with your kids, better.

Do you see why naming a singular priority matters? You're no longer stuck wondering what to do, especially when confronted with a difficult choice. Now you know.

Name what matters most. Make it as singular as you can.

Next, do something about it.

Don't get fooled, though. Don't create a big system or set of rules about your sleep. Instead, make your singular priority into a **smaller choice.**

If you simply say, "Sleep matters most during this next season of life," you'll still be left floundering because "sleep" is too big. You need to make that singular priority smaller.

What are the possible choices that would help you get better sleep during this season? Going to bed or waking up at a different or more consistent time, setting boundaries around your phone usage at night, changing when you shower or when you select what to wear the next day, using a sleep app or white noise machine, learning to sleep on your back so you don't always wake up in pain, or asking your kids to wake up your partner instead of you if they need something in the middle of the night.

That's a lot of possibilities, but don't do them all. Consider what smaller choice would be the most beneficial during this season and focus on that choice only. Maybe it's your phone. Maybe you're like me and sometimes can't turn it off even though your eyelids are made of cement. For this season, a cutoff time for your phone could be a small choice with immense impact.

This is why smallness is so lovely. If you go into a season of late nights and long travel and just hope for the best, the best will not happen. But if you proactively name that going to bed without your phone for the next six weeks is of greatest benefit to your sleep and therefore to every other priority—family connection, energy, creativity, focus, and so on—you will find it much easier to go without your phone for this limited stretch of time. *Because it matters.* And it's small enough to see how much.

That's **proactively** naming what matters.

Reactively Naming What Matters

When a choice needs to be made right now, I want you to focus on one of two things: either trusting your gut or trusting what already matters.

Some situations are circumstantial, which means they need a gut choice. For example, your kid is late getting out of practice, so your evening plans are collapsing like a house of cards. What do you do? You ask what matters most right now and simply answer the question.

As you wait for practice to finally be over, maybe you realize you're angry at your kid, even though they had nothing to do with practice going long. If you're a parent, I have no doubt you've taken something out on your kid that wasn't their fault; I know I have. In that reactive moment, maybe what matters most is taking a few deep breaths while you wait so your kid doesn't feel your misdirected anger. That's one possibility.

Another could be that you're not angry at all, but you are *hungry.* So is the rest of your family, waiting at home. In that case, feeding the crew as quickly as possible matters most. So you pivot from your plan of frozen lasagna (why do they take so long?!) and call home to ask someone to get out tortillas and start grating cheese for quesadillas.

Ask what matters right now and just go with your gut.

Thankfully, you occasionally get to react to a challenge that exists because of your current season. And if you've already proactively named what matters in that season and your gut is weirdly silent, you can lean on an answer you've already named.

If your season of life is fall sports season, when every kid gets home at a different time, dinner can be a huge challenge. What matters most? The answers are plentiful, but let's say you already chose togetherness. Not homemade food, not vegetables every single night, not variety . . . togetherness. By naming this ahead of time, you won't get bogged down with what to make because the point is just to eat food together. Your reactive decisions will follow an easier path. If you're getting home too late to make lasagna, no worries. Togetherness has already been given top billing, and as long as that happens, you can eat anything.

When you have to make a decision in the moment, remember to either trust your gut or trust what already matters. But keep asking the question: **What matters right now?** It's the foundation of everything.

Next, let's build on it.

TO RECAP

You live differently from season to season, making particular choices depending on where you are. All of that begins by naming what matters in the season you're in.

Notice if you are naming what matters proactively about something you already know to be coming or reactively about something that showed up unannounced. Proactively name what matters by first making it singular and then making it smaller. Reactively name what matters by either trusting your gut or trusting the priority you already named.

The most transformative thing you can do is regularly name what matters to you in the season you're in.

4. **Here's The PLAN**

Now we're entering the part of the book where you choose the red pill or the blue pill. The Barbie heels or the Birkenstocks.*
Now is when you consider what you thought you knew about time management and decide if you want to stay there or learn the truth and try something different.

But first, let's review what you're constantly being told:

Time is controllable! You can craft a life where all your goals come true! Simply dream big and don't give up! Never be satisfied with second best! Stay focused! Be disciplined! If you don't have a life you love, you're not trying hard enough, or maybe you've chosen the wrong path! But don't let anyone else tell you if you should change your path! You are the creator of your destiny! You have to outwork everybody else! You can do everything you set out to do! You can fulfill all your dreams!

Turns out "the good life" is made of motivational cat posters.

---

*These references are from *The Matrix* (1999) and *Barbie* (2023), and I refuse to make fun of you if you haven't seen either. Logic, however, tells me you've seen at least one. Also, Weird Barbie for life.

And you feel its flimsiness. You know something is off, but you can't quite place it. You can see the glitch in the matrix.

Still, you don't have an alternative, so you follow the path of productivity: Set purposeful goals, design a plan to get you there, follow it exactly every single day, and eventually you will have a smooth, satisfying, possibly even epic life.

But the reality is that smooth turns bumpy on a dime because something disrupts your carefully constructed plan: hormones, a moody kid, a boss making you work late, a global tragedy you feel powerless to alleviate, a benign post on Instagram that makes you feel terrible about yourself, the discovery that your teenager did not actually do the homework she said she did, the audacity of a three-way stop, freaking *loneliness* and *grief* and *death* and *heartache*.

You can't put those things in a life optimization plan.

As Oliver Burkeman, the author of *Four Thousand Weeks,* puts it, "When you're trying to Master Your Time, few things are more infuriating than a task or delay that's foisted upon you against your will, with no regard for the schedule you've painstakingly drawn up in your overpriced notebook."[1] Oliver, you're killing me.

When that delay is something deeply human, emotional, or outside your control, the system falls apart.

When that delay is something deeply human, emotional, or outside your control, the system falls apart.

And yet we're told that when we hit that bump, that delay, that inconvenience, our linear plans must stay in place. "Stay dedicated," the experts say. "Be disciplined. If you give up now, what kind of person does that make you?"

I don't know, Mr. Expert, but based on your tone, I'm guessing it isn't good.

So even though you're physically exhausted, emotionally wiped, and possibly shedding uterine lining, you are expected to work the plan. You force yourself onto the treadmill. You wash the dishes because experts say to wake up with a clean kitchen. You journal or meditate or lay out your outfit because you said you would.

And if you don't, you are the problem.

Now, I don't want to knock commitment or discipline. Both are great. And maybe for you, they work. Maybe you're glad you stayed committed, and now you wait for tomorrow to do it again. But a lot of people have different experiences. I sure do.

I don't feel satisfied when I force myself to push through, ignoring what I know to be right in my body. If I'm at the end of a day and have unchecked items on my to-do list, I might reluctantly choose to complete them, but I resent it because I really just want to go to bed. Finishing the list never feels like it's *for me.*

But if I do decide to quit the plan, whether for tonight or forever, I don't resent the plan. I resent myself because I wasn't disciplined enough to do what I said I would do.

And guess what happens next?

I buy another planner. I try another system. I read another book. I stay on the machine whose sole purpose is to keep me there.

That's the glitch in the matrix. You keep thinking that one more try will get you there. One more hack, book, course, app, or journal will put you on the path everyone else seems to be on.

Listen to me right now. That path isn't real, not for you and me. It's not worth chasing because we were never meant to catch it.

Not only is the system not for us, the actual mechanics aren't even that great! Linear planning is not resilient. It's not made to withstand disruptions or be nimble. Your choices are **all** or **nothing,** and if you choose **nothing,** you clearly don't have what it takes.

What a vibe.

Still, it's no wonder we believe it, even in part. We've been taught implicitly and explicitly that the best way to be a person is to seek greatness through an imagined future and stay the course no matter what. In some ways, that's the American dream.

And while that dream might occasionally work for a select few, I'd like a different dream. My guess is you would, too. That's why you're reading this book. So let's do it. Let's find a different dream.

Allow me to introduce you to The PLAN.

The PLAN: Our New Time-Management Lens

PLAN is an acronym, and my whole life has been leading up to this because I was an English major and have acronyms and alliteration in my marrow. Please let me have this.

PLAN stands for **prepare, live, adjust,** and **notice.**

As a reminder, there are thirteen Lazy Genius principles, and while all are important, four in particular offer a clarifying outlook for The PLAN.

1. To **p**repare like a Lazy Genius, **go in the right order.**

2. To **l**ive like a Lazy Genius, **live in the season.**

3. To **a**djust like a Lazy Genius, **start small.**

4. To **n**otice like a Lazy Genius, **be kind to yourself.**

If you **prepare** without going in the right order, you will burn out. Guaranteed. Let's learn to prepare without being exhausted.

If you **live** like your entire life is ahead of you, obsessed with where you're going, and show no consideration for your current season of life, you will miss the very thing you're chasing. Let's learn to live without missing our lives.

If you **adjust** with big moves, big swings, and big systems, they will not work. Let's learn to adjust one small step at a time.

If you **notice** and observe your life with eyes of judgment, shame, and guilt, you will never grow into an integrated, whole-hearted person. Let's learn to notice ourselves, our lives, and each other with kind, compassionate eyes.

Speaking of noticing, the first thing I want you to notice is that this is not a sequential acronym. You don't follow the words in a particular order. In fact, these four words are too intertwined and have too much reciprocity to be separated. They're a team. Team PLAN!

But PLAN is not just an acronym. It's also a pyramid. Mnemonics *and* diagrams, baby! We learn with visuals, and I hope you like this one.

If PLAN is a pyramid, its base is what we just discussed in the last chapter: **what matters most in your current season.** Everything rests on that and always, always will.

The three triangles (or pyramid faces, if you're a math nerd*) are **prepare, adjust,** and **notice.** They rest equally against each

---

*Actually, if you're a real math nerd, you've already commented that this isn't a pyramid but a tetrahedron. You're right. PLAN Tetrahedron doesn't exactly roll off the tongue, though.

other, finding support from what matters in this season, and they create the apex of our pyramid . . . the *point*. And the point, my friend, is to **live.**

Everything is in support of living well right now, and even though that's what we really long for, it's not typically what we focus on. We're tied up with striving for perfection, dwelling on the past, or preparing for the future. We're never where we are because that's never been the point.

Until now, instead of orienting our lives around living in this season, in this moment, we've been thinking about what was: what we did wrong, what that person said to us the other day, what life might have looked like if we had taken that other job.

Or we're thinking about what could be: what activity we're doing after this one, what we can do to prepare for that future event better, what life we could have if we weren't stuck with this one.

Our present rarely gets our full attention, and I invite you to begin changing that for yourself.

Theodore Roosevelt's daughter Alice—quite the subversive herself—said she'd "always lived by the adage, 'Fill what's empty, empty what's full, and scratch where it itches.'"[2] Even though her life is fascinating enough to be a prestige television series that I would love for someone to make, she nailed it on the idea of tending to precisely where you are.

Fill what's empty. Empty what's full. Scratch what itches.

But how do we actually *do* that? With The PLAN.

We'll dive deeper into the full acronym in the next few chapters, but first I'll share a metaphor that has transformed my thinking about planning and productivity.

Painting, Not a Puzzle

Living is painting a picture, but we've been taught it's assembling a puzzle.

I love puzzles, but my life isn't one. I'm not trying to repeatedly create a static image, meticulously putting its pieces in place, starting with the edges and working my way in.

Instead, I want my life to be like the act of painting.

I hold my palette, full of all kinds of colors: moods, needs, simple hopes for the day. Then I take my brush, work with what I have, and paint. Depending on what I notice in the painting, I adjust the color. I pay attention to what is happening right in front of me and slowly usher in a beautiful image.

Living where you are is like painting. Not assembling a puzzle. Not even paint-by-numbers. It's painting: fluid, open, creative, and human.

> # Living is painting a picture, but we've been taught it's assembling a puzzle.

Now, lest you assume painting comes easily to me, let me assure you it does not. I am in the 99th percentile of Successful Life Puzzlers. I can craft an impressive "You Are Here" map the likes of which you've never seen. Puzzling has been my default for decades. But being good at puzzling doesn't mean it works. Robotically constructing your life to match the picture on the box is unsustainable.

Nor do I think you really want to keep that up.

So instead of trying so daggum hard at something that you might not even want and that definitely doesn't work, let's paint.

If you think in the abstract, you'll love this. If you find even doodling to be outside your comfort zone, hang tight—specific, helpful words are coming. Regardless of how much or little this idea resonates with you, it still rings true.

Life is a painting, not a puzzle.

TO RECAP

The PLAN is our new lens for managing our time.

It is an acronym **(prepare, live, adjust, notice)** and functions as a structurally sound pyramid, with the three faces **(prepare, adjust, notice)** resting equally against each other to support how we **live**.

The interplay of these four words, all on the beautiful

foundation of what matters right now, is the architecture of your days and therefore your life. Not a life that's perfect or without struggle or loss, but a life that is vibrant, rooted, and whole and gives you the freedom to be who you are.

As you conceptualize your life this way, remember that living is like painting, not like putting a puzzle together. Your new goal of integration means being flexible with whatever colors you have in front of you, and your focus on today means not requiring a picture on the puzzle box to work toward.

Let's talk about how to paint with The PLAN.

5. **How to Prepare**

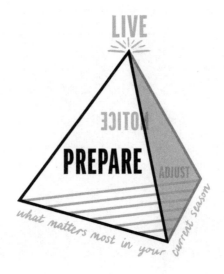

This is not a chapter about dying, but that is where we'll start.

Oliver Burkeman posits that our culture is obsessed with productivity and the future in part because we're afraid to die. "It's only by facing our finitude that we can step into a truly authentic relationship with life."[1]

That'll preach.

We're not a culture comfortable with death. We don't know

how to sit in the discomfort of losing control, losing loved ones, losing our very life. So we ignore the reality that our lives are just a breath in the wind and instead, as a distraction, focus on giving structure to an invisible future.

And yet today is full of time. Beautiful, wondrous, finite time. Still, we spend hours and hours and days and days of it on *preparation,* on getting some kind of hold on a future we cannot control. We do this because it's what we've been *taught* to do.

If you examine Western productivity down to the marrow, you'll find *the future.* Every hack, tip, strategy, and system prepares us for what will come. We're making choices now to live the life we want later.

Now listen. I am not critical of looking ahead. Looking ahead is my *favorite.* In fact, one of the thirteen Lazy Genius principles is **ask the magic question:** *What can I do now to make something easier later?* I love thinking about the future!

But if getting ready for our future comes at the expense of our present, we will always feel discontent. We will continuously struggle to truly live our lives because we're not *really here.* Preparation cannot be our primary focus.

> **If getting ready for our future comes at the expense of our present, we will always feel discontent.**

The hosts of my favorite podcast, *The Popcast with Knox and Jamie,* often ask if something in pop culture is overrated, underrated, or properly rated. Using that rubric, preparation has been traditionally overrated. Like, *aggressively.* In order for preparation to be properly rated, it has to be part of a larger story, not the main character.

So, as we dive deeper into this new idea of preparation, you should know you're not going to get a tidy list of hacks. Life hacks are full of puzzle energy, and we're painters. Here's how to prepare with that in mind.

The Right Order for Everything

To prepare like a Lazy Genius, you go in the right order.

In many cases, it's not that you're doing the "wrong" things; you're just doing them in an unhelpful order. That's why **go in the right order** is one of the thirteen Lazy Genius principles. We need the reminder.

While some things have a very specific right order,* here is the general right order for situations big and small:

1. Name what matters.

2. Calm the crazy.

3. Trust yourself with what comes next.

This is the foundation of preparing like a Lazy Genius, so let's make sure you understand it.

1. Name What Matters

Naming what matters in your current season is the base of The PLAN Pyramid for a reason. If you ignore what matters to you, you'll have no way to discern what you should do next.

---

*Like cleaning bathrooms, making soup, and the order in which to read the Throne of Glass novels.

Name what matters in this moment, in this conversation, in this event that's coming up, in this disappointment, in this hiccup in your organized schedule. If you need a refresher, reread chapter 3.

Whatever it is you're doing, always begin with what matters.

2. Calm the Crazy

Because the productivity industry has a lot to say about preparation and you've probably spent much of your adult life distilling and integrating it all, it's natural for preparation to feel overwhelming.

Instead of allowing that frantic energy to run the show, focus on calming the craziest part. Wherever you are, in whatever you're planning, notice what feels the most overwhelming. What is turning your brain to mush? What has you running for the hills? *That* is where you want to focus your energy, not on big preparation systems.

For example, if I'm preparing to go to a family reunion, I might think my stress is because I'm taking a big trip. A decent thought, right? But maybe not. "Taking a big trip" is quite broad. So instead of staying overwhelmed, I go in the right order. I name what matters to me about this trip, which is to feel like myself and have a nice time. But I begin to realize that while I do love these people, they tend to argue as a recreational sport, something that does *not* allow me to feel like myself or have a nice time. And now I've pinpointed the real problem. The real source of my stress is anticipating confrontational conversations. What a gift to know that! Now I don't have to waste my time trying to find a new packing system or creating a color-coded travel itinerary, neither of which will help because organization is not really the problem. Instead, I can begin calming my anxiety about the real issue. Beautiful.

And now the final step in going in the right order.

3. Trust Yourself with What Comes Next

It always astonishes me how, after I've calmed the crazy, my mental capacity to make a decision skyrockets. Suddenly, I'm a person with a rational brain and space to see my situation more clearly! But can I trust my solution? Can I trust what I think should come next?

Unfortunately, this is weirdly challenging, especially for women. Let's talk about it.

You Can Trust Yourself

Men, in general, don't struggle with trusting themselves. They just do the thing, and if it's wrong, they'll try again.

As women, we have a different hurdle. Our voices have been diminished in more spaces than you might realize, and our confidence has been systematically undermined.

> # Our voices have been diminished in more spaces than you might realize, and our confidence has been systematically undermined.

Remember, the system wasn't built for us.

In diet culture, women are told we can't trust ourselves around foods that will make us gain weight, so we need to clear out literally everything that might tempt us.

In some areas of Christian culture, women are told to defer to men and that a woman's judgment should be reserved for homemaking and childcare.

According to a 2022 study on women in the workplace, women in leadership roles are leaving their jobs at rates higher than we've ever seen, and much higher than men are, in part because women are "twice as likely to be mistaken for someone junior and hear comments on their emotional state."[2]

As a kid, I was told a woman can't be the president of the United States because she would be too emotional to effectively lead, and I know I'm not the only one with that kind of upbringing.

In every context that has a hierarchy rooted in patriarchy, women have historically not been valued, trusted, or believed.

It's tough to see the core of who we are, what we want, and what we can beautifully offer the world when our insides have been painted with a thick coat of deference and dismissal.

We're always in danger.

We aren't strong on our own.

We can't be trusted around Oreos.

We don't really understand "how it's done here."

We don't have an innate sense of direction or sharp reflexes, so our husbands should drive.

We can't expect a guy to not be a guy when we wear a dress like that.

We can't be sure of the difference between consent and rape.

I'm not using sexual assault as a casual, dismissive example to make a point on time management. Traditional Western society's assumptions about women and the expectations put upon us are necessary considerations as we explore what it means to live our lives well. I believe it is *imperative* that women recognize that the challenges we experience over something as simple as preparing for the next day started before we were even born. We have been breathing the air of the patriarchy our entire lives and don't even see the disregard we experience on a regular basis. We can't seem to trust ourselves because no one else does.

Now, if your experience is different, if you grew up in an empowering home and you have flourished as an adult in environments that honor your voice and your strength, I am genuinely grateful that's your story. For most women reading this, however, that's not how the story goes.

Empowerment for women has not come easily. We've had to cheer ourselves and each other on. We've chosen to believe in our own worth through whatever spiritual or faith lens we have. We've had to come at it from that direction because our offices, families, neighborhoods, churches, courtrooms, and boardrooms have not been reliable places to have our voices consistently heard, honored, or believed.

Which is why you sometimes have trouble trusting yourself.

I will now tell you that you can. You *can* trust yourself.

Will you get it right all the time? No. No one does. Will you sometimes have incomplete information and wish you had made a different choice? Of course you will. Will you be swayed by others' opinions, choices, and needs? Get in line, pal.

But that doesn't mean you are inherently untrustworthy. It just means you're human like everybody else.

So, when you are preparing for a situation, no matter the stakes, take comfort in going in this order: Name what matters, calm the crazy, and then *trust yourself* with what comes next.

Three Mindsets as You Prepare

The PLAN Pyramid works because of its inherent balance. All three faces are equally important, working together to support how we live. But sometimes we put too much emphasis on one, creating an imbalance that topples our beloved pyramid. And that is especially true with preparation.

To prevent that from happening, each face of our pyramid, each word in our acronym, has strong boundary lines in the form of three essential mindsets.

Here they are for *prepare:*

1. Not everything can matter.

2. A plan is an intention, not pass-fail.

3. External solutions will not solve internal problems.

Let's look at each in more detail.

1. Not Everything Can Matter

You cannot be a genius about everything. You cannot have a robust, joyful, meaningful existence in every arena at once, at least not according to the culture's measurements of what that should be.

You can't do everything, you can't be everything, and you sure as hell can't do either perfectly. Unfortunately, this unrealistic expectation is still perpetuated in the productivity industry.

So even though you know this and sometimes even live this, I still want to remind you that *not everything can matter and that's okay.* In fact, let's normalize letting certain things go for the sake of doing what matters most. The more we do that in community, the more we encourage and inspire each other to pursue true *living.*

So when you prepare, remember that not everything can matter. Prioritizing is good. Delegating is good. Releasing is good. Doing what matters to you right now in this season *is good.*

2. A Plan Is an Intention, Not Pass-Fail

In the old productivity paradigm, when you make a plan for whatever day, event, crisis, project, goal, or conversation is in front of you, it's very easy to see it as pass or fail: Either every part works and you pass, or even one thing doesn't and you fail. Even if you have a more reasonable approach and say that a 70 percent success rate is still a pass, that evaluative practice will wear you down. Plans are not meant to be pass-fail.

> # If your plan works, it works. If it doesn't, it's not a failure. Neither are you.

Plans are intentions. Preparation is putting things in place for later with the expectation they will work, but sometimes they do not. I'd like to say that we can separate the plan being a failure from *us* being a failure, but I don't have much evidence of that. Women are under a lot of pressure to be perfect, to get it right. When something doesn't happen the way we hoped, we blame ourselves. We feel guilty for not doing better, for ruining the experience of someone else. We obsess over every detail or every word to see where we went wrong and try to ruthlessly eliminate those mistakes next time. We evaluate and grade ourselves just like we do our plans, and that is not the way it should be.

As I said, a plan is just an intention. How you prepare is neutral. Do what makes sense for you by going in the right order, and if your plan works, it works. If it doesn't, it's not a failure. Neither are you.

3. External Solutions Will Not Solve Internal Problems

External solutions aren't bad. I'll even give you a few in this book. Still, pay attention to the true source of your problem before attempting a solution.

If you're struggling with preparing dinner, you might create a new meal prep system to make it easier. But somehow it's not easier. You get progressively more annoyed at the process and yourself, but you push through it anyway. What if it's not about the system? What if it's about your insecurity or guilt over how often or how well you cook dinner? No number of cute bento boxes or meal plans will change how you feel inside if you don't acknowledge what's actually happening.

Now, I'm not saying you have to be completely at peace with your inner challenge before you can apply external strategies to it. They can run concurrently. They often do. But you can't ignore what's happening on the inside and expect things to get better.

As you prepare, *notice.* (See? We haven't even gotten to the *notice* chapter, and I already have to bring it up! Team PLAN!) Notice when you feel off. Notice when you're frustrated, bored, unkind to yourself, scattered, or overzealous and those feelings kick your preparation into overdrive. Chances are you need a tune-up on how you see preparation itself, and these mindsets can help you get there.

Now let's talk about what it means to **live** right where you are.

TO RECAP

Preparation is familiar and can trip us up, causing us to prepare in the old way, with the invisible future as our guide. Instead, remember your finitude. Life will end, and no amount of planning and preparation can change that.

Instead of focusing on the preservation of your life, focus on *living* it with these three mindsets: Not everything can matter, plans are intentions and not pass-fail, and external solutions will not solve internal problems.

And in all things related to preparation, go in the right order: Name what matters, calm the crazy, and trust yourself with what comes next.

---

6. **How to Live**

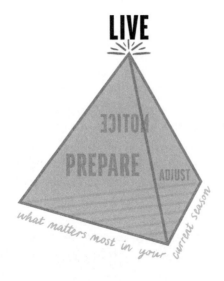

I don't know whether to laugh or cry about needing a chapter on how to live, but here we are.

Frankly, I thought I already knew. You probably did too. Living is a pretty basic concept, right? Shouldn't be too hard.

How cute.

In my twenties, I lived like I could do everything—and failed. In my thirties, I leaned into that failure and lived by doing almost nothing. In my forties, I'm learning to live in the balance between the two. But that doesn't mean the balance is obvious to even the most eager eyes. Remember, we live in a productivity-industrial complex within a digital, capitalistic society. Inputs are overwhelmingly numerous, and we're taught to take in as many as possible with efficiency, optimization, and success. As I've already stated, I don't think that's really living.

The Power of Right Now

If you think back to the spring of 2020, to those early pandemic days, we had to relearn how to live. I know I did. As an entire population, we suddenly went from processing every input in our lives to having hardly any at all. It was wildly unsettling, especially at first.

In their children's book about the pandemic, *The Great Pause,* Julia Manini and Anne-Joyelle Occhicone write, "The whole world was busy being busy, too busy. And so, they did not notice; they did not breathe deeply, and they did not pause. Until something happened to one person, then to another, and then to the whole world. And it was as though everything just stood still."[1]

The stillness eventually became my preference, but it took a while for me to get there. For weeks, I could not calibrate to this slow, delayed way of living. My brain literally didn't know what to do.

Note: Before I go on, I need to make an important disclaimer. Our family's pandemic experience was challenging but in a very particular way. We were exceedingly privileged during those months, and I don't want to communicate anything different. My husband is a school counselor, and I am an author and a podcaster. When the stay-at-home order came down, he and I were both fortunate enough to be able to work from home. Our kids did online school, and we had the resources to get everyone their own screen. We started doing grocery pickup because we had a car and could. Kaz and I have lived in the same city a combined eighty-seven years with deep roots and relationships, preventing us from experiencing the kind of stark loneliness so many dealt with. We didn't lose anyone during those awful separate days and therefore didn't experience the isolated grief forced on so many.

Although our experience wasn't easy, we had a tremendous amount to be thankful for, namely that our road was paved with only emotional challenges and manageable ones at that. I'm sincerely sorry if your road was marked with more challenges.

Those first few months of the pandemic forced a slowness and contentment upon our family, one that I desperately needed to experience. I suddenly had space for tender, quiet, thoughtful moments. I read Wendell Berry. I painted mediocre flowers and drew pictures of trees. Our family played games and baked bread like the rest of the country. I had no choice but to give in to the slowness because there was nothing to be busy about.

There was also nothing to plan for. The future was unsure and a little scary, and testing positive for Covid-19 could happen at any time. It could not have been more pointless to plan ahead.

It was in that release that I realized how little attention I paid to exactly where I was.

Previously, I mostly focused on what was coming, on how to make life better, and my present generally served my future. Occasionally, that's helpful. I even think I was fairly healthy about it. Before the pandemic, I had already given up on trying to do it all for the sake of doing what matters, and I enjoyed my days. But only to a point.

Thankfully, that point hit home during those still months, and I saw what I had been missing. I saw *right now.* Once I had tasted it, I didn't want to lose it again and vowed (maybe like you did) that I would not go back to the way things were. I would stay present and slow, still and content, satisfied and happy. I would be right where I was.

A worthy goal but one that is hard to hold on to once life picks right back up again.

However, I've made a dent. I love nurturing the practice of being right where I am, thanks to the perspective I got when the world came to a halt.

But wouldn't it be nice to find that perspective without a global catastrophe? This is why in order to really live, you must live in your season.

> # In order to really live, you must live in your season.

Your season defines your needs, your needs affect your priorities, and your priorities inform your choices. If you're not aware of your season, life becomes too unwieldy, too spread out, too unmanageable.

You can't live well if you don't pay attention to where you are right now.

But here's a quick pro tip: The smaller you make your season, the easier it will be to PLAN and therefore live in it. That's why the pandemic felt so overwhelming, even through our newly opened eyes. We didn't know how long the season would last. We thought it would be small, that the end was around the corner, but we went months and months (and months and months) before seeing any sort of end.

Enormous seasons feel unending. Intellectually, you might know that life won't always be this way, but it sure does feel like it will. That's why making your season smaller offers help and hope.

Let's look at parenting as an example. Parenting is a season.

A long one. And assuming your kid outlives you, parenting will never really end. Does it shift? Of course. Most seasons do. But we get so deep in the weeds of our own lives that we can't always recognize that our *right now* is more manageable than we think.

Let's make the large season of parenting a smaller one and see what happens.

- Parenting

- Parenting a middle schooler

- Parenting a middle schooler who just got a phone

- Parenting a middle schooler who just got a phone in the summer

- Parenting a middle schooler who just got a phone in the summer while I'm trying to finish up a work project over the next three weeks

Do you see the difference? If you say you're in a hard season of parenting, that is head-shakingly too big. You can't find easy solutions for something that size. But if you say you're trying to parent a middle schooler who just got a phone and is using it in a way you don't love but work has you too busy to be as involved as you'd like? That's an entirely different animal.

It is the most natural thing in the world to see your current season as one large, unending stretch of time, so make it smaller. Name the season you're in and make it as small as you can. The smaller the season, the easier it is to PLAN.

Three Mindsets as You Live

Just like with preparation, **living** needs its own boundaries to keep it from getting out of whack, so hold tight to these three mindsets:

1. Do not judge every day against your best day.

2. Contentment is the antidote to optimization.

3. You're allowed to care.

Let's look more closely at each.

1. Do Not Judge Every Day Against Your Best Day

When you have a really great day where everything is flowing, your people are happy and compliant, you get your stuff done, and somehow you still have time to sit down at the end of the day and do something fun, a cosmic force compels you to replicate everything you did today and make it happen tomorrow.

> **It's normal to want to have a good day. Maybe even the *best* day. But if your best day becomes the measurement for all other days, you've already lost.**

I did this with my kids when they were tiny. If one of them took a magically long nap, I would move heaven and earth to meticulously copy every decision I made that particular day in the hopes I could get the same nap the next. It was like I was counting macros but for time.

It's normal to want to have a good day. Maybe even the *best* day. But if your best day becomes the measurement for all other days, you've already lost.

Not only that, but "the best day" probably equates to "successfully executed plans," and I'm not sure that's the rubric we want.

When you spend time crafting a plan and everything works, it is such a rush. I will never argue otherwise. But the assumption is we should live with that kind of logistical high every single day or, at the very least, keep striving for it.

We have diminished *living* to *getting things done.*

> # We have diminished *living* to *getting things done.*

We're cranky at the end of the day because of "what went wrong." We're frustrated and discontent that things don't feel as easy as we think they should. We wonder where we messed up, because it never used to be this hard.

You didn't mess up. You've just been using the wrong kind of ruler.

On the day I'm working on this chapter, I'm supposed to be on a writing retreat in my own home while Kaz and the kids visit family one state over. As luck would have it, two of my four precious people got strep throat mere hours before they were supposed to leave.

I should be alone right now, working at whatever pace my creativity dictates, but instead I'm writing in fits and starts as I tend to my physically sick and emotionally sad family. No one on planet Earth would say I'm having the best day.

But through a very specific kind of lens, I am.

Over the last few years, I have slowly become more integrated, and today that integration has manifested itself as contentment, patience, and flexibility during a challenging time.

Am I disappointed my family isn't eating dinner somewhere else while I enjoy some kind of spicy noodle situation none of them would touch? Yes. Am I having a mild crisis over whether I will finish this book on time? Sort of, but I also know that I will. Is my current circumstance one I would've chosen? No, this is definitely not a choice I'd make on the verge of four days *alone in my own home*.

Yet I feel good. I have pivoted well, and I am at peace. I ordered groceries, I arranged for a couple of fun things to lift spirits over the next few days, and I am sitting in my chair writing. Will I have to get up in approximately nine minutes because someone will need something? For sure. And four minutes is probably more accurate anyway. But I'm proud of how I'm moving through this. Years ago, I would've been in a resentful ball, wondering why all the terrible things happen to me. Today, even a bad day, is still a pretty good day.

Stop judging every day against your best day, and ask yourself what *best* means anyway.

And . . . a kid just texted me needing something. Three minutes.

Let's move on to our second mindset for living.

2. Contentment Is the Antidote to Optimization

There is so much pressure to optimize ourselves into the ground, and we can't seem to figure out how to stop.

Enter **contentment**. Contentment is how we stop, at least for as long as the contented moment holds us there.

When you're trying to improve, rush, or change something, it means you're not content with how it is. In some areas, that's important, like surgery and bridge construction. In other areas, though, it's a distraction.

You and I have both experienced nights on the couch with a pen and paper in hand, laptop propped on our legs, writing down all the things we need to improve in our lives and then googling to find ways to make them better.

But where does that compulsion come from? Is it from the deepest, truest part of you? Or does it come from a culture that tells you that no matter what you do, it's probably still not enough?

What if you were to nurture a sense of contentment in your life? Not complacency, not apathy. Contentment. You see things for what they are, and you're able to **live** there with compassion and kindness. That, by nature, is at odds with optimization.

Practice contentment and you'll definitely live well.

This brings us to our third mindset for living.

3. You're Allowed to Care

The temptation is to swing from one extreme to another, from "I can do everything!" all the way to "I don't do *anything*." And while that might offer satisfaction for a short time with all its Boss Babe/Hot Mess energy, it leaves you with little room to pursue what matters to you. Just because you've spent a lot of time trying to be everything to everyone, it doesn't mean your only option is to throw in the towel on living a life you love.

You're allowed to care! Love what you love. Develop skills. Seek knowledge. Hone a craft. Enjoy a hobby. Care about things! Don't assume that taking the blue pill or putting on Weird Barbie's Birkenstock means you don't care anymore.

You're allowed to care. Even deeply. Obsessively. Put forth tremendous discipline and commitment if that makes you more yourself. Caring is not proof of still being on the productivity machine. Caring about what you want to care about is a sign of being integrated.

Now let's look at what happens when things feel a little off and you need to **adjust.**

Caring is not proof of still being on the productivity machine. Caring about what you want to care about is a sign of being integrated.

TO RECAP

As you *live,* remember to live in your season. Where you are right now is the most significant place you can be. You can make that season more manageable by making it smaller and naming what matters to you exactly where you are.

When life goes haywire, remember the three mindsets for living: Do not judge every day against your best day, contentment is the antidote to optimization, and you're allowed to care. This is how you live well.

7. **How to Adjust**

Let me introduce you to Big Black Trash Bag Energy.

Big Black Trash Bag Energy is the frenzied frustration that everything is falling apart and the only way out is to completely start over.

It's throwing away your planner in surrender and starting a bullet journal.

It's getting so annoyed with your kids' lack of help around the house that you proclaim, "Things are going to be different around here," as you start hanging chore charts on every wall.

It's feeling stressed about a work project and spending all evening scrolling job sites.

It's putting on a swimsuit that's tighter than it was last year and throwing away all the food in your house that's not from the earth and signing up for a smoothie delivery service.

It's the sudden visceral desire to set your house on fire and live in a van.

It's grabbing a literal big black trash bag and filling it with your family's junk that you warned them to put away or you'd throw it out.

Big Black Trash Bag Energy is not an adjustment. It's a massacre.

And on top of being expensive, both financially and emotionally (children often cry when you throw away their toys), Big Black Trash Bag Energy simply doesn't work.

Sure, it works as a release for your anger, but once you run out of steam and pass out like an overstimulated toddler, the problems remain. Not only that, but now your toys/planner/cookies are on their way to the dump.

Throwing everything out in order to clear the decks and start over seems easier in theory. It's that "You Are Here" map again. Build it from scratch! We can make it whatever we want! Endless optimism! That is, until it's time to make dinner in a kitchen that's midway through a clutter purge or to get dressed when most of your clothes are now at Goodwill. Giving in to Big Black Trash Bag Energy doesn't seem so fun now, huh?

But the antithesis of the trash bag massacre, of that "go big or go home" perspective, is something we really, *really* do not like. It's to start small.

"But, Kendra, noooo! Starting small is too slow, too ineffective, too inconsequential for the chaotic garbage dump I'm living in!" I get it. You want a challenging situation to get fixed immediately, and anything that takes time is the worst. I would yell at me, too.

However, one of the smartest, most effective skills you can learn is how to **adjust,** and in The PLAN, we do that by starting small.

I Know You Hate It, but Start Small Anyway

Start small is one of the original thirteen Lazy Genius principles, and she is easily the most annoying of the group. She knows it, I know it, we all know it. But she is also the most helpful.

When you start small and adjust only one challenge at a time, two things happen.

One, you eventually have a solution or system that actually works over time because you've been fine-tuning day after day instead of starting over every six months.

My family has a fairly seamless weekday morning routine. Everyone knows what they're doing (with kind prompting from their mother, of course), no one is frantic, and most of us get out the door with everything we're supposed to have. Was it always like that? What an adorable question. Zero percent. But *over time,* I have made small adjustments to our mornings, eventually landing on a morning routine that has been working for us for several years now. Will it always? Probably not, because seasons change, and that'll be okay. Go for the long haul, not an overhaul.

> **Go for the long haul, not an overhaul.**

Two, you learn to *trust* small steps by starting small.

Those of us in Western culture don't have a lot of practice at small steps. We tend to create one giant system (enter the Big Black Trash Bag approach)—often informed by the latest productivity book we've read or podcast episode we've listened to—and live with it until it breaks down and we can't take it anymore.

We simply do not adjust well, and we definitely don't trust those adjustments when they are small. Incremental adjustment is not a skill we practice, and it's not a skill the industry widely promotes.

The messaging from the white guys without bosses is along the lines of "*This* is how you structure your workday" and "*This* is how often to check your email" and "*This* is how to do everything you want in only four hours" and "*This* is what you should eat for maximum energy" and "*This*" and "*This*" and "*This.*"

Plus, they all start with the future, with that "You Are Here" map they're meticulously constructing: "Where do you want to be in twenty years? What needs to happen in ten years to get there? Five? Two? One? Okay, now let's break down those goals into quarterly tasks, and then spread those out over the next twelve weeks. Now work the plan."

In some ways, this is smart. You won't ever get to that twenty-year goal without breaking the path down into smaller and smaller steps. But you started from the invisible future of greatness, not from where you are right now. You tried to be great before just *being.*

I've always wanted to be a real artist, to paint or draw something beautiful every time I tried. Then I realized that's not what a real artist is. A real artist learns to *trust* the process, the small steps of learning how this color mixes with that one, how this brush makes one mark and that brush another, how holding the pencil one way creates a line you can't get otherwise.

The more you patiently take small steps, whether in your

work, your hobbies, your relationships, or your home, the more you experience how trustworthy they are. Small steps can be trusted. Small adjustments lead to true change.

You will not live a full life by breaking a future goal into small steps and putting your nose to the grindstone until you get there. A full life happens within the confines of where you are currently, within the life you already have. Goals are great; we'll talk about them later. But they are not where we begin.

Start where you are and adjust with the strength of small steps.

Three Mindsets as You Adjust

When you're struggling to adjust with small steps, these three mindsets can help bring balance again:

1. Match your expectations to the energy you're willing to give.

2. Now isn't forever.

3. You're allowed to change your mind.

Let's look at each in more detail.

1. Match Your Expectations to the Energy You're Willing to Give

How many times have you watched a professional athlete who has meticulously, diligently trained her body to do what she does and then beaten yourself up for not looking like her? Even though you have not moved your own body in an eon, you suddenly expect yourself to work out thirty to sixty minutes every day so you'll look like an Olympic beach volleyball player in three months.

Girl. *No.*

Going from *nothing* to *everything* is not a sustainable jump. Big changes require big moves, and big moves require big energy. My guess is you don't have a lot of that to go around.

Still, you try. You pick something you want to do, or think you *should* want to do, and create a big plan to make it happen. All too soon, you discover that your expectations of how you want your home, schedule, meals, body, yard, and friendships to be are in egregious conflict with the energy you need to fulfill them.

> # If you don't have the energy, adjust the expectation.

So, when you're adjusting a situation, possibly more aggressively than you know is helpful, remember to match your expectations to the energy you're willing to give. If you don't have the energy, adjust the expectation. It doesn't mean you're giving up. You're simply naming what matters based on where you are right now.

Here's the second adjust mindset.

2. Now Isn't Forever

Adjustments are small not only in scope but also, potentially, in duration. You can make an adjustment in your PLAN that is for just today or just this week, knowing full well it won't stay like that forever.

That's not an easy thing for our "set it and forget it" culture. You've been striving so long for a robot life, where you pull a lever and everything seamlessly connects, that you forget you can choose something for *right now.* Something that works today doesn't have to work tomorrow. Now isn't forever.

This mindset is also in conflict with the standard approach to time management, where the choices you make every day are leading you to a singular point two decades down the road. For years, I believed that if I made an adjustment that served me today but conflicted with a future goal, I was being irresponsible and wasting time.

While that mentality might be true for some, it definitely is not for me and probably not for you, either.

I want to live my life *right now.* I don't want every choice today to be inextricably linked to my retired self . . . if I'm even able to live that long. Yes, I am investing money in a retirement account. Yes, I am renovating a bathroom that I hope I'll love for another couple of decades. Yes, I am doing things with the future in mind.

But the future is not in charge.

Nor am I locked into a forever decision by choosing something different today. If I am on a book deadline, it's okay for my family to eat hot dogs and spaghetti on the regular, even if that's not my ultimate preference, because now isn't forever. Adjust based on what matters to you *right now.*

On to our third adjust mindset.

3. You're Allowed to Change Your Mind

Decide once is one of the original thirteen Lazy Genius principles, and it is what it sounds like: *Make one decision one time about one thing, and then keep doing that thing until it doesn't work anymore.* A while back, I decided to wear the same thing— black jeans and a chambray shirt—on Mondays because the day was stressful enough without having to figure out what to put on. I wore my Monday uniform for five years. I wrote about it in *The Lazy Genius Way,* I was tagged in posts about Monday uniforms on Instagram, I was asked about it during podcast interviews . . . the Monday uniform was a whole thing.

And I no longer do it.

I changed my mind.

Sometimes things work for a season and then just don't anymore. Sometimes you try something and you don't like it. Sometimes you discover a different option that you like better.

You're allowed to change your mind.

> **Sometimes things work for a season and then just don't anymore. Sometimes you try something and you don't like it. Sometimes you discover a different option that you like better.**
>
> **You're allowed to change your mind.**

I can totally hear you energetically saying that you change your mind all the time and it's not good! Or maybe that you worry you're just not sticking with something long enough! Or that you're not disciplined enough to follow through on your choice!

Deep breath.

Remember a couple of chapters ago when we talked about

trust? About how women have been raised to not trust themselves? This is that.

You're allowed to change your mind.

Will you always get it right? No. Is every choice a right or wrong one? No. Are you a trash human with no discipline because you decided to do something else? No.

There will be times when you change your mind too soon, too late, or in an unhelpful direction. Of course there will be. We're humans, and we don't always make the best call.

However, you're still allowed to change your mind. You might end up backpedaling a bit as you **adjust,** but the actual choice of changing your mind? You can absolutely do that and not feel bad about it.

Next, let's talk about **noticing.**

TO RECAP

Say goodbye to Big Black Trash Bag Energy. Start where you are with those annoying but effective small steps and adjust from there. The more you choose to adjust with small steps, the more you organically build systems that work and the more you trust a slow, small process in the first place.

As you adjust, remember the three mindsets that help you do so in a thoughtful, kind way: Match your expectations to the energy you're willing to give, now isn't forever, and you're allowed to change your mind.

8. **How to Notice**

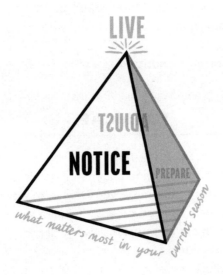

We're excellent at noticing. It's just that we often notice the wrong things.

Depending on your story, your personality, and your life stage, you probably notice unhelpful things all the time, like if you have enough of something: favor, power, money, knowledge, safety, fun, control, peace, credibility. Or maybe you notice if *you* are enough as a partner, parent, boss, employee, friend, child, sibling, neighbor, writer, reader, planner, leader. Both lists never end.

The unhelpful thing I tend to notice is what's right and wrong, but not in the way you might think. Somehow, in my sweet little perfectionistic brain, I seem to always know the *right way* to do something, even when I don't have the skills, experience, or knowledge to back it up. It's such a delusional vibe. And yet if I notice without kindness, a delusional vibe it remains.

When you notice without kindness, nothing good comes of it. You are judgmental toward others. You are ashamed of yourself. You resent your season of life. You compare yourself to strangers on the internet. Honestly, judgment doesn't notice anything that matters.

> # When you notice without kindness, nothing good comes of it.

Again, such a vibe.

That is why **be kind to yourself** is the Lazy Genius principle we lean on here.

Just like we **prepare** by going in the right order, we **live** in the season, and we **adjust** by starting small, we **notice** by being kind to others and ourselves.

As we further explore The PLAN and what it means to notice, I encourage you to remember kindness. Be kind and compassionate to yourself as you try and fail. Be kind to others as they live differently than you do. Be kind. Be kind. Be kind.

Notice the Right Things

Noticing the right things isn't just about noticing what's beautiful in life. Sure, I want you to notice sunsets and flowers and the way your friends laugh. In fact, as I'm sitting here on this Airbnb couch right now, a female cardinal is perched on the power line right outside my window, and she's lovely. These are things to notice and hold. But I'm talking about something a little more specific.

I want you to **notice** how your implementation of The PLAN is going.

Not react, not judge, not assess. Just **notice.**

> # Noticing isn't swooping. Noticing might lead to swooping, but they are two different things. And honestly, not everything needs a swoop.

A lot of people notice something wrong and quickly swoop in to fix it. I am absolutely one of those people, and we are great in a crisis. I have witnessed a car accident where bodies were okay but anxieties were not, and I pulled over, got out of my car, and asked the trembling teenage girl who was at fault if I could hug her because her body needed to know she was safe. She said yes, and I squeezed this sweet stranger for a full minute and helped steady her breathing until the police arrived. I am for sure a swooper.

Noticing isn't swooping. Noticing might lead to swooping, but they are two different things. And honestly, not everything needs a swoop. You might notice something that could be better, but it's not your problem to solve. You might notice something in your own life you'd like to be different, but you need to temper your immediate reaction to it or else you'll end up holding a Big Black Trash Bag.

Simply practice paying attention and notice where you are.

Notice your preparation and if it seems to be helping. Notice to what extent you're living where you are. Notice a place that could benefit from a small adjustment.

Notice your mood, your hormones, what your body is telling you. Notice if you're feeling excited, fearful, frustrated, or empowered. Notice your patterns of behavior and if you might learn something from them. Notice what worked in the past, how you felt about a decision, or what made you happy in recent days.

Noticing is vital to your PLAN because it's your check-engine light, not a five-alarm emergency. You are not steamrolling. You are not making immediate changes. You are not observing your life from ten thousand feet up in a disembodied way. You are slowly learning to respond to the cues of your body, your environment, and your people and to honor what those cues are telling you.

Notice **kindly.**

Kind eyes aren't focused on the immediate fix. Kind eyes don't bring judgment into the conversation. Kind eyes recognize the value of waiting. Kind eyes see your human self instead of pushing you toward that whole robot vibe we're actively trying to avoid.

Be kind to yourself as you notice what's happening in your life.

Three Mindsets as You Notice

If you find yourself noticing your life but not in a kind way, lean on these three mindsets:

1. Staying grounded is better than staying on task.

2. Your body is wise.

3. Good is here right now.

Let's explore these.

1. Staying Grounded Is Better Than Staying on Task

Typical productivity culture would scoff at prioritizing staying grounded because staying on task is *everything*. Maybe you feel the same and think I'm being ridiculous and unrealistic.

> *If poop is on the floor from my kid's unruly bowels, you want me to focus on staying grounded instead of cleaning it up?*
>
> *If my work deadline is in an hour and I still have five hours of work left, you want me to focus on staying grounded instead of hustling to get it done?*
>
> *If we all just got home from a long day and everyone is starving, you want me to focus on staying grounded instead of making actual food?*

Yes.

Staying grounded doesn't preclude staying on task. But if you try to stay on task in a frantic state, you will not stay on task for long.

Also, remember the foundational principle here: Be kind to yourself.

When you focus on staying on task at the expense of your own mental health and your own calm and your own humanity, that is decidedly unkind. And yet we do it all the time.

Take a deep breath. Access kindness toward yourself and others. Remember what matters. Completing the task can come after. I know this feels counterintuitive, but do it anyway.

Staying grounded is better than staying on task. They can exist at the same time, but being grounded is decidedly better both for your soul and for actually getting the task done.

> **Staying grounded doesn't preclude staying on task. But if you try to stay on task in a frantic state, you will not stay on task for long.**

2. Your Body Is Wise

The camp is divided on this one.

I've heard a disheartening number of people over the years say they do not believe the body is wise. It can't be trusted, it's separate from who you are, and it doesn't have anything significant to say.

You are allowed to hold your own opinions without my judgment, and we can totally disagree. But I will say that I think you're wrong. Granted, it's not your fault that you're wrong, because we are an extremely disembodied culture. But I think you're wrong.

I believe that your body is wise. It understands what you need.

For years, I did not listen to my body. I would go hard, hustling to get everything done, even the good things, and my body kept tapping me on the shoulder to tell me, in the form of fatigue, headaches, and shortness of breath, to slow down. I rarely listened, so my body had to get louder.

Consequently, every few weeks, I felt like I had the flu. My head and stomach hurt, I was tired and achy, and I would usually need to poop and then crash for twelve hours. It was like clockwork. Very disturbing, annoying clockwork.

At first, I thought it was hormones, and it was, to a point. I was moving at a constant pace with no variability, and my hormones are too variable to support that. (We'll get into that in the next chapter.)

But really, my pace was the perpetrator. My body had quietly been telling me to slow down, at least occasionally, but I wouldn't listen. Instead, it had to get so loud I had no choice.

Your body is wise and will tell you what you need to know. It's part of how you notice what's working, what you need, and what matters.

If your body is tired, find a way to let her rest. Adjust your priorities to create space. Prepare differently for tomorrow so you can honor what she's telling you. Live in the season you're in with kindness so you can respond to your body's wisdom.

As licensed therapist Hillary McBride says in her book *The Wisdom of Your Body,* "Being fully connected to the body is about being fully alive."[1]

3. Good Is Here Right Now

This is what separates noticing from reacting.

Good is here right now.

When you say that good is here right now and—better yet— **believe it,** your reaction time is blissfully slower.

You can notice a mess in your home without jumping into Big Black Trash Bag Energy because there is good in that mess. You can lie next to a sick kid and not resent her for ruining your plans because good is in this sweet moment. You can enter a new stage of life without falling apart because you have eyes to notice that good is in this unique season.

Is every situation amazing? Unlikely. Are there seasons that are so difficult you don't know how you'll get through them? Yes. I've been through a few myself.

But grounding yourself in this mindset while you struggle is a gift. It prevents you from being swallowed up by your experience. Good is here right now. If you can notice the tiny bit of good and breathe into it right where you are, you will process the past and future and manage the present more kindly.

TO RECAP

Notice the right things by noticing with kindness. Don't immediately swoop. Allow the space between noticing and reacting to create spaciousness inside you.

If you feel like your noticing needs a tune-up, remember your three mindsets: Staying grounded is better than staying on task, your body is wise, and good is here right now.

Remember that this mindset is new. Starting where you are to live a life of integration isn't formulaic or linear. Remember, life is painting, not putting together a puzzle, and The PLAN is the beginning of your artist's palette.

Notice with kindness. Adjust one small thing. Prepare in the right order. Live in your season. Build your PLAN on what matters to you right now.

Our goal is integration as we start where we are. You're doing great.

9. **Let's Talk About Periods**

We can't talk about time management without talking about periods.

For women, there is an inextricable link between the organization of their time and the management of their hormones, and if we try to live detached from that link, we will feel the consequences. Unfortunately, we're *expected* to live detached from that link.

Since most productivity authors don't have a menstrual cycle, most productivity books don't talk about it. In fact, hormonal fluctuations aren't even a consideration. Instead, women are told to manage their time and live their lives according to the same rhythm and rules that men do, but we literally *cannot.*

Men have a twenty-four-hour cycle, so their energy levels are reasonably consistent day to day. Dare I say this is why they are so hubristic in their advice on what a person can control. When you're not bleeding from your body for days on end or regularly hit with spikes of progesterone that cause you to feel like you can't even stand, I suppose it's a little easier to predict your life.

Women are on, approximately, twenty-eight-day cycles, not twenty-four-hour ones. Our hormones fluctuate week to week, which significantly affects our energy. Is that taken into account in our jobs, our healthcare system, and even our personal relationships? Not really. We're just being "moody," and our "time of the month" becomes a punch line.

The intersection of time management and a woman's hormones is an opportunity for empowerment, efficiency, and empathy, but sadly that intersection is ignored, and at the most impactful time of a woman's life, too.

> **During their busiest years, most women experience monthly hormonal changes— yet we completely ignore a woman's hormones in time-management conversations.**

Think about it. When are most women the busiest? From their twenties to their fifties. They're building careers, establishing credit, starting relationships, raising kids, managing households, and a million other things. And during their busiest years, most women experience monthly hormonal changes—yet we completely ignore a woman's hormones in time-management conversations.

Our support systems and productivity resources are woefully incomplete.

This is yet another reason why your time-management struggles are not your fault. Our culture was not built for, nor does it adequately support, a woman's variable hormones, whether you have a typical or an irregular cycle, are on birth control, or have gone through menopause.

The way a woman's body uniquely works *matters,* and I want it to get its spotlight.

First, let's look at why we're here in the first place.

What Women Are Up Against

As early as 1900 B.C., the inconsistency of a woman's moods and energy was blanketed under the word *hysteria.* It's based on *hystera,* the root word for *womb,* and was perpetuated by Hippocrates (Greek physician "Hippocratic oath" Hippocrates) in the fifth century B.C.

That was a really, *really* long time ago.

Hippocrates claimed that a woman's hysteria was due to the "abnormal movements of the uterus in the body."[1] In other words, he (and therefore everyone else of note) believed that the uterus was literally moving around inside a woman, causing pain and emotional instability. For a time, the only cure was to "anchor" the uterus in place with pregnancy. How does one get pregnant? Sex. Just keep having sex, ladies. We won't comment on who primarily benefited from that.

Eventually, the narrative moved from hysteria to women being witches, which, to be honest, isn't the greatest upgrade, and 250 years ago, a woman's cycle was seen as demonic.[2] Super chill. Granted, 250 years was quite a while ago, but the field of women's health has not made nearly as many strides as other areas of medicine. It is limping along and far behind. Just look at the design of the speculum.

This lack of progress has been more devastating for women of color. Black women in America were treated as disposable objects when they were enslaved, and that horror continued even after slavery was "over." Today maternal mortality rates of non-Hispanic Black women are three to four times higher than those of non-Hispanic white women because of the implicit bias against and disregard for their health and wellness.[3]

Frankly, women don't receive enough support, understanding, or empowerment from our existing cultural systems, which are steeped in a history of dismissing our bodies and their needs altogether. It's an uphill climb.

I do believe the road is getting cleared. More women are becoming doctors and seeking to improve women's health, not just to uphold a faulty system. There's more comprehensive, inclusive medical research on things like endometriosis, menopause, and hormone replacement therapy. The needle is moving. It's moving slowly, but it is moving.

However, it can move faster in the area of time management. We don't have to wait for medical trials and lab tests. We can simply change the narrative.

Aligning Your Hormones with Your Life

There are four phases to a woman's cycle, which *thrillingly* line up with our PLAN acronym *and with the seasons of the year.* Seriously, can we handle it? Patterns everywhere.

A woman's hormonal patterns, and therefore her energy, vary multiple times over a single month. If, as a woman, you start to *notice* those patterns and *adjust* your decisions based on the energy you have, you will *prepare* differently and therefore *live* the way you desire to live.

There are several authors who have written fantastic books on the menstrual cycle, and some of their observations were instrumental in the writing of this book. Kate Northrup, the author of *Do Less,* says we should manage our *energy,* not our time.[4] I'm so grateful for such an important, simple distinction.

I also first learned about the alignment of the menstrual cycle with the seasons of the year from Maisie Hill, the author of *Period Power.*[5] The following pages are the result of my synthesizing their expertise with the structure of The PLAN.

Let's get into it.

> # If you start to *notice* those patterns and *adjust* your decisions based on the energy you have, you will *prepare* differently and therefore *live* the way you desire to live.

The Menstrual Phase/Winter—*Notice*

Days 1 to 5*

This is when you bleed. A delight.

But this is also when you are slower, you retreat, and you easily notice what's happening in and around you.

Winter is your model. In winter, nature slows down. It rests. It moves inward. And when you are in your menstrual phase, so do you.

As much as it's in your control, during this phase each month, don't be overly social. Do mindless, slow tasks like paying bills,

---

*These ranges are approximate. Some women's cycles are like clockwork, and others seem to be based on a broken sundial. Wherever you land, feel free to adjust your days accordingly.

folding laundry, and filling out spreadsheets. Make comforting dump-and-stir dinners. Go to bed earlier on these days and take advantage of the rest your body naturally craves. Don't expect a lot of creativity to come out of you. It's on a break right now, and that's expected and part of your rhythm.

This is the time you **notice.** You don't react or fix. Just notice. You're primed for it, so let it do its beautiful work.

The Follicular Phase/Spring—*Prepare*
Days 6 to 12

Now things start to grow, namely estrogen and the energy she brings.

You have more elasticity in your creativity and more clarity in your ideas. Curiosity, strategy, and even patience feel readily available to you . . . because they are. There's a groundedness and hope in this phase, where you feel like something is possible *and* you have the energy to figure out how to make it happen.

You are excited to **prepare.**

During this phase, take advantage of your curiosity and clarity of thought. Write or do deep, focused work. Organize your closet, make travel plans, decide dinner for the next month, house-hunt, and create a product launch strategy.

Look at your beautiful, unique life and identify what you could prepare for. Then kindly and wisely use your natural abilities to do it in a way that honors your season of life.

The Ovulation Phase/Summer—*Live*
Days 13 to 18

Listen up because you need to pay attention to this phase.

From a physiological standpoint, this is the phase where your body is trying to get pregnant. Therefore, it's the most open and attractive you'll ever be to others.

Let's set aside actual impregnation for a moment and recognize that this phase is when you're the most *alive.* You are open, engaged, and fully yourself more than in any other phase. You likely experience an uncommon ease when you walk into a room. It's not that you're loud and super social; you're just *you.* Purely, uniquely, beautifully you.

I want you to keep an eye on this phase. It's the shortest one (some say it lasts only the two to three days when you actually ovulate), but I believe it's the one that you need to intentionally lean into. Take advantage of being comfortable with who you are and find ways to be around people. Speak with the confidence you suddenly feel in the conference room. Invite your coworker or neighbor to lunch. Have friends over for dinner even though you're usually terrified to do that. Schedule interviews, presentations, and parties during this phase. Live like it's the best summer of your life.

We all want to feel accepted, to confidently walk into a room without evaluating whether or not we belong there, but that assuredness is sporadic for many women. What a gift it is that every month, your hormones enable you to experience that confidence. You get to just **live.**

The Luteal Phase/Fall—*Adjust*

Day 19 until your period starts

It makes sense that after a few days of socializing and feeling alive with possibility, you need to wind down a little. The luteal phase of your cycle offers a natural opportunity to experience that.

This is a great time of the month to make space for tasks that are detailed and need a keen, grounded eye—tasks that need **adjustment.** Evaluate household and workplace systems and identify a small change to make the systems more effective. Clean the bathroom, edit the manuscript, make the more complicated recipe, and schedule performance reviews.

You're naturally inclined to see ways you can adjust in a direction that matters.

People Without Periods

What if you are a woman who is on birth control or who's going through perimenopause or menopause? Can you still experience these phases and rhythms? To a point, yes.

A birth control pill does affect the balance of hormones in your body and the rate of their release,[6] so it's likely that the energetic swings are not as pronounced if you're on the pill.

If you're in perimenopause or have already transitioned to menopause, your hormones have started to rest in new places. The fluctuation eventually becomes less intense because your body has adjusted to no longer being viable for pregnancy. However, the process to get there is varied, long, and often deeply discouraging for women. There has been very little research on the symptoms and results of menopause, and consequently women have few resources and limited understanding of what to even expect. As the endocrinologist Susan Davis says, "Women are frustrated that they're trying to function, and no one knows how to help them."[7]

Despite these variations in hormonal release and a woman's experience of the cycle, this rhythm of **prepare, live, adjust, and notice** is real. It exists in a woman's menstrual cycle but is also mirrored in the seasons, the natural creative process, and even the phases of the moon. What a gift to hold this cycle in our bodies, too.

Now that you know how to leverage your natural energy, let's talk next about what it means to bring your whole self to the table.

TO RECAP

A woman's body is amazing. The hormonal advantages women have are just that—*advantages.* But in order to use them wisely and well, we need to know they exist and believe that they are good.

You're not hysterical, and you don't have to be embarrassed by the fact that you're bleeding. It's like pooping. Everybody does it. Well, almost.

You can allow this knowledge to influence and improve how you live day to day, leveraging your cycle to your energetic advantage.

10. **Bring Your Whole Self to the Table**

I used to spend my Friday nights taking personality tests.

While my high school peers were out seeing *Can't Hardly Wait* (or going to parties that loosely resembled the movie *Can't Hardly Wait*), I was in the personal growth section of my local Barnes & Noble, excited to use my Chick-fil-A paycheck on self-discovery. I would snatch up six-dollar leaflets that were meant for professional performance reviews, not for a high schooler in thrift-store overalls, to find out, for example, how well I communicated with others. Twenty-five years later, that interest in self-discovery has not changed. I *love* a quiz. I mean, BuzzFeed just said my *Harry Potter* personality is Fred Weasley, and here I am thinking I'm Hermione! How will I know who I am unless someone else tells me?

While BuzzFeed might not be the best lens for psychological evaluation, I do think there is value in naming who you are. Factors including, but not limited to, your personality, upbringing, current physical and mental health, and faith practices all contribute to the way you live your life each day. These innumerable inputs naturally affect how you spend and manage your time, which is why the concrete systems in the personal growth section of the bookstore don't comprehensively work. None of those resources can accurately capture everything you are and everything you need to live an integrated, fulfilling life.

This book can't do that either.

I cannot create a system that works for every person. No one can. We're all too different, not just individually, but even *day to day*. Depending on my hormones, how poorly I slept the night before, and how long it's been since I've hung out with a friend, my days vary. Yours do, too.

> # What you bring to the table today is likely different from what you brought yesterday and what you'll bring tomorrow. It's not exceptionally different but different enough to make a difference.

This is why we skip the puzzles and paint instead.

A puzzle is fixed with the same thousand pieces no matter when it's assembled, and we assume the same is true of our lives. It's not. What you bring to the table today is likely different from what you brought yesterday and what you'll bring tomorrow. It's not exceptionally different but different enough to make a difference.

Your circumstances themselves might not change. In fact, depending on your season of life, you might feel like Bill Murray in *Groundhog Day,* living in a nauseating state of repetition. But what we bring from *within* ourselves, affected by a wide variety of outside influences like sleep, world news, or a comment on Instagram, changes all the time. Even if our circumstances stay relatively consistent, our days are rarely identical.

I find this to be comforting. It means I'm **living.** Fluidity is absent from "set it and forget it" time-management systems, and I want women especially to embrace the beautiful movement we naturally possess.

In short, be more flexible with what you expect of yourself each day. You are always living from a shifting spectrum of energy and resources, and I want you to kindly and wisely account for that shift. Your palette of "colors" is dynamic, not static, and that's an exceptional thing.

As the wise philosopher Genie from *Aladdin* once said, "Beeeeeee yourself."

Let's consider some of the different ways *you* might come to the table.

Personality

Your personality is the unique combination of characteristics and qualities that make you *you.* How many of your characteristics and qualities do you think you could name? That's not a trick question. I wonder how well you can articulate who you are.

A lot of women I know are quite self-aware, but they tend to verbalize the negative qualities over the positive ones. I once asked a roomful of women, "What do you like about yourself?" and you could hear a daggum pin drop. Then one woman said, "No one has ever asked me that before." As we say in the South, that is a cryin' shame. But it would not take you more than ten seconds to get a woman to tell you something she's bad at. Maybe closer to five.

I'd like that to change.

This is why I love personality tests. They offer language to speak more confidently about ourselves. My favorite framework is the Enneagram,* but I also love Myers-Briggs, Clifton StrengthsFinder, and unscientific *Harry Potter* quizzes. Knowing more about myself helps me recognize how I move through the world *and* how I might sometimes consider moving through the world differently as I pursue a grounded, integrated life.

For example, the Enneagram has helped me see how good I am at solving problems. It honors that about me. It also shows me how judgmental I get when I'm cranky and where the twain meet.

If my husband is solving a problem in our house in a different way than I would, I have learned to hold back a little, to not swoop in and fix what I think is broken. Kaz is just solving the problem the way he wants to, and that's okay. (It's less okay when I'm cranky, but we're working on it.) If I didn't have that language about myself, I would just keep swooping and fixing and judging, and my marriage would suffer because of it. I don't want that. I want a healthy, loving marriage, and understanding my personality moves me in that direction.

Lest you worry this is a performative box to check, knowing who you are doesn't mean you'll always be the best version of yourself. It just means you're bringing your whole self to the table, no matter who that self is today. Certain Kendras have to apologize a lot, and others will hug you after a car wreck. And guess what? They're all me. You also have multiple versions of yourself, and the more you understand your unique personality, the more integrated you become.

But integration is not the only benefit. Knowing yourself makes you better at The PLAN, too.

Let's imagine our PLAN Pyramid. As a reminder, we live with

---

*Suzanne Stabile is my favorite Enneagram expert, and *The Enneagram for Black Liberation* by Chichi Agorom is one of the best Enneagram books.

the equal support of **prepare, adjust,** and **notice**. However, none of us are naturally good at all three. Like, nobody. I have no data to back this up, but I will still stake my house on it.

> # The more you understand your unique personality, the more integrated you become.

One of the three likely feels easier to you, and I say lean into it. But don't lean so far that you forget the other two. You need them all.

If you **notice** what is stressful about your life without ever making **adjustments** or **preparations** for what you're seeing, your stress is going to manifest itself as passivity and with-drawal. Instead, pay attention to how you might **prepare** a bit ahead of time or learn to **adjust** a bit in the moment. You're capable of developing new skills.

If you live in a constant state of **adjustment** without any form of **preparation** to stave off problems or without **noticing** what the problems are in the first place, you will run yourself ragged, jumping from one crisis to another. So, if you feel like you're constantly putting out fires, even if you're good at it, consider amping up the **notice** and **prepare** sides of your pyramid. You're capable of developing new skills.

Finally, if you put all your energy into **preparation** but don't **adjust** when you hit a roadblock or **notice** the life that is hap-pening around you, you'll probably be fairly pissy most of the time. There's nothing worse than a prepared woman scorned. But guess what? You're capable of developing new skills.

Each person is naturally inclined to **prepare, adjust,** or **notice,** and I want you to stay connected to what you're already gifted in. Name it. Embrace it. Be confident in what you're good at. But don't let that come at the expense of the other two. Your practice is to learn which one of the three is most dominant and then nurture the others. Over time, you'll find yourself more present to your life.

Get to know your personality and bring the fullness of who you are to the table.

Neurodiverisity and Mental Health

Let's talk about executive function skills.

Executive function skills are the mental processing abilities that help you get things done, things like planning, managing time, focusing, following directions, and breaking a large task into smaller pieces. Unfortunately, the cultural assumption is that everyone is cognitively on a level playing field, and that could not be further from the truth.

KC Davis, a licensed therapist and the author of the excellent book *How to Keep House While Drowning,* writes, "ADHD, autism, depression, traumatic brain injury, and bipolar and anxiety disorders are just some of the conditions that affect executive function, making planning, time management, working memory, and organization more difficult, and tasks with multiple steps intimidating or boring."[1]

In fact, some people require up to a hundred times more mental energy to plan compared with people whose brain chemistry naturally aligns with traditional planning.[2]

One hundred times.

And this isn't just about a small handful of folks. The National Institute of Mental Health estimates that 4.4 percent of adults have diagnosed ADHD, which is about one out of every twenty-five people.[3] Additionally, a 2023 Gallup poll found that 17.8 percent of Americans were suffering from depression,[4] and according to the World Health Organization, depression is about 50 percent more common in women than in men.[5]

Those are some bummer statistics.

And yet they offer such clarity.

If you live with a diagnosis that affects your executive functioning—or if you are in a season of situational depression because of a death in the family, a health crisis, a divorce, or any number of other personal events—traditional time-management strategies that are based on high levels of executive function will be more difficult, if not impossible, for you to access.

My mom had a nervous breakdown when I was in third grade, and when a family friend tried to explain to me what that was, she said, "Your mom doesn't know how to make a sandwich." I remember thinking that was so strange because everybody knows how to make a sandwich! But her executive function skills were so impaired that her brain couldn't figure out the steps to put something between two slices of bread.

If you struggle with staying on task, getting things done, or being organized, there is an excellent chance that your executive function skills are working at a diminished capacity. It's not that you're lazy or unorganized or a hot mess. Your brain chemistry or circumstances simply make those skills more difficult to access. I hope knowing that is freeing.

Bring that knowledge about yourself to the table. Not everyone is capable of or even interested in being "good at" time management, and you can start where you are and go in the direction best suited for you.*

---

*Numerous neurodivergent folks as well as licensed therapists have told me that the thirteen Lazy Genius principles found in *The Lazy Genius Way* are quite helpful for people with diminished executive functioning. I'm not an expert, but you could give it a try. If you want a resource by an expert in ADHD, try *Scattered Minds* by the physician Gabor Maté.

Faith and Spirituality

Spirituality in any form is essentially a framework for how to live, so what you believe is integral to how you make decisions, view others, and show up in the world. Some faith traditions have spiritual practices and even calendars that affect your daily life, and it's vital to bring this part of yourself to the table.

For some, myself included, faith isn't just part of who you are; it *is* who you are. It's the foundation of everything: the backdrop, the backbone, the air you breathe. Your faith is so connected with your life that trying to disconnect from it feels like death.

Faith and spirituality often illuminate *why* you want to live in the first place.

Part of the reason I crave a time-management system that's not about my greatness is that my faith rests on the greatness of God, not on me. Being great sounds absolutely exhausting, but it's also against what I personally believe. I believe in humility, that the first shall be last, that power is not mine to hold. God is the one who gets to be great, and thankfully I just get to be God's.

Even the idea of starting where you are has faith implications for me. I pray for daily bread and rejoice in the day that the Lord has made. The words of Jesus himself remind me that I should not worry about tomorrow, for tomorrow will worry about itself; that the birds of the air and the flowers of the field have their needs met, so how much more must the God of the universe care for me and mine. There's even the devastating line "Who of you by worrying can add a single hour to your life?"[6] What a mic drop.

If we think back to living being like painting, your faith or spiritual beliefs could be a color on the palette. For me, it *is* the palette. Or maybe it's the brush. I don't know, metaphors are weird. Either way, if you are a person with faith or spiritual practices, be sure to bring that part of yourself to the table. It might carry a lot of weight.

Hormones and Other Things Beyond Your Control

We just discussed the illustrious menstrual cycle in the previous chapter. Sometimes you love it, sometimes you hate it, but it is part of your whole self. No matter what your hormones are doing on any given day, pay attention to how they're influencing today's version of you.

Then there are other things beyond your control. The fitful night of sleep because your partner snored, the offhand comment from the stranger at Target that you're still thinking about, or sudden tragic news.

We simply don't know what might suddenly throw us off.

I still remember how I felt in late May 2022 after the shooting at Robb Elementary School in Uvalde, Texas. For days, I was practically catatonic after taking my kids to school. I couldn't do *anything.* The darkness I felt was so oppressive I could almost see it. Every school shooting is a devastating tragedy, but for whatever reason, I felt that one in my bones and did not know how to cope.

Everyone experiences unexpected situations where they just don't know how to cope. It could be *big coping* like a senseless war or *little coping* like losing your favorite pair of earrings at the park. Clearly, I'm not saying those two situations are the same, but our bodies and emotions often respond to unexpected situations in unsettling, even debilitating, ways.

My invitation to you is to be kind to that version of yourself and bring her to the table. No matter what is happening in your uterus or in the world, you can show up the way you are *today,* even if it doesn't make sense.

TO RECAP

You cannot create an ideal day and live it out until you die. You are not putting together the same puzzle ad nauseam. You are a unique person with a layered personality.

You might have a brain chemistry that prevents you from practicing the normative version of time management. You might struggle with a clinical or situational mental health challenge that affects your ability to make a grocery list. *You might be bleeding from your body for five days.* (Seriously, why does no one acknowledge how cuckoo pants this is.)

You are who you are, and the more you learn about her and honor her and lavish kindness on her, the more you will experience a wholehearted, integrated life.

Learn to embrace every color on your palette.

11. **Manage the Right Thing**

The full title of this book is *The PLAN: Manage Your Time Like a Lazy Genius,* but time isn't the only thing to manage. In fact, if your primary focus is managing your time, you're flirting with living like a robot.

People who desire a life of integration instead of greatness need a more comprehensive perspective on what we're truly managing. Fortunately, that perspective lines up perfectly with our PLAN acronym, except we're going in a different order. I'm the author and I'm allowed to do that.

Notice your energy.

Adjust your expectations.

Prepare to pivot.

Live together.

It's NAPL instead of PLAN, but I still think the alignment is cool.

Let's examine all four.

Notice Your Energy

You've already learned a chapter's worth of information about how a woman's hormones affect her energy, so we won't go into that here. But even beyond your menstrual cycle, noticing your energy still matters.

You might wake up with one energy and fall asleep with another. Energy has its own agenda. The point is not to predict it or manipulate it to stay the same throughout the day. The point is to *notice* it. Will you probably make adjustments? Sure. Will you anticipate tomorrow's energy based on how today went and prepare for it? I think that's great. But ultimately, practice noticing first.

One way to notice something is by giving it a name, which is true of energy, too.

When you wake up in the morning, as you're drinking your coffee or taking a shower or making breakfast for your kid, see if you can name your energy. Use the seasons, animals, a character on a TV show . . . choose your own adventure. Just name it.

My son Ben is emotionally intelligent beyond his years, and when he was in elementary school, he told me that his feelings were a rainbow. Red was the happiest, and purple was the saddest. Now when he's feeling his feelings, I can ask, "What color is your heart right now?" He'll answer, "Dark yellow," and we go from there.

Maybe you can use Ben's rainbow. Or build on it by adding an animal on the end of the color: "Today, I'm an orange sloth. I'm feeling pretty good, but I'd rather not move."*

---

*This is a great daily practice for little kids, by the way. Help them cultivate the habit of naming how they're feeling and honoring it as you go through your day.

Whether you name it or not, notice your energy. Allow that to influence how you manage your time.

Adjust Your Expectations

One main objective of traditional productivity is to master your day in order to reach optimal greatness and success. You now see the holes in that paradigm, but that doesn't mean its impact has disappeared. Many of us still feel that if we follow the right plan, life should work out. We subconsciously *expect* a baseline of success. Consequently, we're annoyed and even discouraged when life doesn't go according to plan.

Instead of being surprised by that reality, change the narrative.

Adjust your expectations.

What you hope for will not always come to pass. What you prepare for will not always work. What you expect might not even be clear until the expectation goes unmet.

> **Pay attention to what you hope for and appropriately adjust that toward a more wholehearted objective.**

I'm not asking you to be Eeyore and assume everything is going to fall apart at every turn. Adjusting your expectations doesn't mean adjusting them in a defeatist direction. I'm asking you to pay attention to what you hope for and appropriately adjust that toward a more wholehearted objective.

You've likely always managed your time, albeit reluctantly, according to the tenets of greatness and optimization, and that ideology inherently includes an expectation of perfection and control. Instead, adjust your expectations toward self-compassion and presence. Life won't always go the way you expect, but that doesn't mean you're doing it wrong.

Prepare to Pivot

If those motivational cat posters have taught us anything, it's that obstacles are a part of life. But I don't always have the energy to hustle past, climb over, or obliterate whatever is in my way. Pivoting sounds nicer, doesn't it?

Here's how I pivot. Maybe you can give it a try.

1. Breathe.

    Yes, it's the most annoying advice, but do it anyway. Breathing calms your survival instincts. It tells your body that this Lego you just stepped on is not going to kill you and that the child who left it there is not a threat. Breathe.

2. Actively seek softness.

    When I am activated by a problem, I tighten up. Sometimes it comes out as anger, pride, or stubbornness, and none of those are helpful. Instead, I actively seek softness within myself. Compassion, empathy, kindness, warmth. Even if the slowness of the customer service rep is making me late for an appointment, I can still be soft toward her. Pivoting is easier when you're pliable.

3. Name what matters.

Look! Our pyramid base is here! Once you've calmed and softened your body, name what matters most in that moment. As you've already learned, doing that *in a specific moment* is easier than you think. Plus, the more you do it, the better you become.

4. Make the problem smaller.

Now that you're calm and soft and have named what matters, you're in a better position to examine the obstacle and make it smaller. Have the missing peas from your grocery order really ruined dinner? Is that the actual problem? Or can you make it smaller? Instead of letting one missing ingredient snowball into burning your kitchen to the ground, name the smallest problem. You need a new side to go with dinner. That's much easier.

5. Solve the problem.

Look at that! You're calm. You're soft. You've named what matters most right now. You've made this huge obstacle into a small and manageable problem. Now solve it. You'll likely know how or have the emotional resources to figure it out.

> **Learning to pivot is more important than learning to plan.**

I strongly believe that learning to pivot is more important than learning to plan. If you take nothing else from this book but these five steps, I consider your investment here fruitful.

Live Together

During the pandemic, I experienced a paradoxical form of community. Besides my husband and three kids and eventually a bubble family or two, I saw no one. Neither did you, I'm guessing. Still, somehow, I felt deeply connected to the other people in my life because *we were all going through the same thing.*

Most of my friends were living the same rhythm in their homes that I was in mine. The adults worked in breakfast nooks and spare rooms while simultaneously helping the kids do online school. By late afternoon, after hours of trying to complete tasks, love each other well, and not murder anyone in frustration, we'd have dinner and just . . . hang out. We played games, baked bread, and watched *Stranger Things.* Occasionally, we'd socially emerge from our cocoons and FaceTime each other or even venture out to stand far apart in front yards just to say hi. Then we'd do it all again the next day.

There were no meetings, no outings, and no distractions. We were living alone but somehow still living together.

I always thought this communal connection was because of this strange, mind-boggling, even traumatic shared experience, and while I'm sure that's partly true, I wonder if another element was at play, one we can incorporate into how we manage our time now.

Let me quote Oliver Burkeman's *Four Thousand Weeks* one more time:

As with money, it's good to have plenty of time, all else being equal. But having all the time in the world isn't much use if you're forced to experience it all on your own. To do countless important things with time—to socialize, go on dates, raise children, launch businesses, build political movements, make technological advances—it has to be synchronized with other people's.[1]

The first time I read that, my brain exploded.
Of course.
Of course time loses its value if we can't synchronize it with other people's. It's not that we don't have time to invest in communities and relationships. **It's that our time doesn't line up.**

This idea gains further importance in *The Good Life* by Robert Waldinger and Marc Schulz, a book that summarizes the Harvard Study of Adult Development, a seventy-five-year scientific exploration of what makes people happy.[2] The simple answer? Relationships.

> **The happiest people are the ones most connected to their families, friends, and communities, but we live in a culture that is becoming more focused on individual time autonomy.**

The happiest people are the ones most connected to their families, friends, and communities, but we live in a culture that is becoming more focused on individual time autonomy. We have dinner and toilet paper delivered. We can go to church online. Even streaming services disconnect us from each other because we're not watching our shows at the same time.

In addition, as Robert Putnam talks about in his book *Bowling Alone,* the disintegration of social institutions—things like civic groups, dinner parties, and bowling leagues—is impacting America's social capital.[3]

We are missing each other with devastating consequences, and the time-management implications are alarming.

As you think about how you want to live your life, especially within this new integrated paradigm we're making for ourselves, I want you to remember the importance of relationships. PLAN like those relationships matter, because according to the longest behavioral study in history, they matter the most.

Where in your current season of life do you notice places that your time lines up with someone else's? Where can you adjust so that you and a friend can do a similar activity at the same time? How can you prepare the rhythms of your life to better accommodate communal time and not just yours individually?

To quote Jack Shephard from *Lost,* one of the last "watch party" TV shows, "If we can't live together, we're going to die alone."[4]

We need to listen to Jack.*

TO RECAP

Our brand of time management is not just about time, is it?

We need to notice our energy, adjust our expectations, prepare to pivot, and live together if we want integrated

---

*Not about tattoos but definitely about this.

lives of wholeness and joy that are valuable right here, right now. If you do those things and never make another to-do list again (don't worry, there's a whole chapter on to-do lists), I believe your life will offer more beauty than you can hold, even when your circumstances say other-wise.

Part Two
Strategies

T

he principles from Part One offered a new way to see. The strategies from Part Two will give you new things to *do.* This is the part where the rubber meets the road.

However, you *can* drive too fast.

As you explore these next few chapters, read them with a discerning eye. I will teach you numerous strategies, all of which are great, but they might not all be great *at the same time.* Trying to apply everything in this book at once is like expecting to go from zero to sixty in three seconds while driving a Ford Pinto. That is neither how that car nor how The PLAN is built. Instead, start small.

As you read, **notice** what resonates and what doesn't, and **adjust** any ideas to make them work for you. Apply a little bit at a time in whatever way works best for you. This section is not prescriptive or linear. It's simply a collection of strategies that kindly align with the principles of The PLAN.

12. **Start with Today**

Now that we're in the strategies section of the book, it's time to get to work, right?

I should help you distill the information you've learned into an action plan with goals, processes, and checklists so that you can be the project manager of your own life and put together the puzzle of your future.

But that is not how we do things. That is not how we live.

Instead, we are painters, and we start with today.

For some of you, that's a strange place to begin. The key to everything is supposed to be your goals and dreams, right? You're used to lines like "If you don't know where you're going, you will probably end up somewhere else" and "You miss 100 percent of the shots you don't take" and "Why do anything unless it's going to be great?"*

I don't know about you, but I do not need the pressure to make everything great.

---

*Those quotes are attributed to the educator Laurence J. Peter, hockey superstar Wayne Gretzky, and organizational consultant and author Peter Block, respectively.

The person reading this book has a different rubric. You're not measuring life by greatness, success, or completed goals. In fact, I personally don't want to "measure" my life at all. I want to *live* it. You're likely the same.

> # I personally don't want to "measure" my life at all. I want to *live* it.

However, at this very moment, you could look up from this book and see the clutter on your counter, the fullness of your inbox, or the laundry on your couch and feel like *living* is a bit simplistic.

You also have to get stuff done.

Which is exactly why we start with today.

Get Familiar with Fragmentation and Urgency

I love this tweet: "I'm writing Spider Ma'am, about a middle-aged woman who gets bitten by a radioactive spider but keeps it to herself because she doesn't freaking need this."[1]

The devastating accuracy.

Women traditionally have more on their minds and plates than men do, so it's only natural that we start where we are. Frankly, today has enough already.

First, let's name why today is so challenging.

The clinical psychologist Joyce Chong says there are five reasons, and I've paraphrased them here:[2]

1. Connection to technology

2. Attempts to do too much

3. Infrequent prioritization

4. Inadequate stress-release mechanisms

5. Sensory pollution (overstimulation, multitasking, decision fatigue, the environment)

This list represents two things that are vital to recognize throughout your day: **fragmentation** and **urgency.** Let's start with fragmentation.

Fragmentation is being pulled in too many directions, often to the point of breaking. A common example is when all three of my kids are talking at the same time, one needing an answer, one needing comfort, and one needing a snack. That is a moment where I experience fragmentation, and it feels like pieces of my brain are now on the floor. Perhaps you can relate. Or maybe you're imagining a day at work where you're trying to do your job, finally focused and on a roll, but then a coworker pings you with a question at the exact moment your boss knocks on your door. You sharply inhale and hold your breath, eyes wide and brows high, a deer caught in metaphorical headlights. That cognitive freeze-frame is caused by fragmentation.

And this experience isn't restricted to the daily grind. Fragmentation exists in pleasant areas, like hobbies, too. Celeste Headlee, the author of *Do Nothing,* puts it scarily well: "Our attention is now nearly always divided, because we seem to be always working on something. Our hobbies have become goals. Our homes have become offices and our free time is not free."[3] If you've ever wondered if you should turn your love of crochet into an Etsy shop, you feel this in your bones.

Frankly, the human brain is simply not made to sustain this kind of wear and tear. In fact, there is research to support that not only is the human brain *not* designed to fragment and multi-task but that consistent attempts to do so change our brain chemistry to a point where we struggle to stay focused on anything.[4]

So multitasking makes us worse at multitasking *and* focus. That's not troubling at all.

Next, let's look at urgency.

Urgency is when something requires immediate action or attention. Um, isn't that everything?

Personally, I feel like something always requires my attention. Whether it's a kid, a task, a text, or even just the urge to check my email again, I could always be tending to something. In truth, those things are rarely urgent.

Consider phone notifications. Not every ping is make or break, and yet we have been trained to respond to those pings immediately. We intellectually know we don't have to, but we do it reflexively anyway—mostly for the dopamine hit notifications and refreshed timelines give us. But the cost is high. When something feels urgent, it triggers our brains to release hormones that cause an elevated heart rate, shortness of breath, and an overall experience of intensity. Hilarious. As if we need more of that.

Our attention is split in multiple directions, and every single one feels urgent. This psychological burden will stick around without some sort of intervention, and I have a couple of ideas that just might work.

Tend to the Necessary Before It Becomes Urgent

Urgency is when something requires immediate action or attention.

Necessity is when something is required or indispensable.

Importance is when something is significant or valuable.

Usually, we start with what's urgent, and for things like re-pairing broken relationships and busted water pipes, urgency is a solid approach. But if you treat everything as urgent, the things that matter suffer. Instead, name what is important about today and tend to any necessary things *before* they become urgent. If that becomes your practice, you will avoid the subsequent personal short-circuiting that is fragmentation.

Not only is this essential for getting your stuff done, but it is essential for your mental and physical well-being. The American Institute of Stress estimates that 75 to 90 percent of all visits to primary care physicians are because of stress-related issues.[5] That is a devastating number, a number that is heavily affected by fragmentation and false urgency.

Name what matters, prioritize what is important, and tend to the necessary before it becomes urgent.

The TODAY Framework

Most people cannot and, frankly, should not approach every day the same way. That's a recipe for unmet expectations and exhaustion. Additionally, planning a single day can sometimes feel too big, let alone planning a week or (gasp!) a month. I have ideas for both in subsequent chapters, but sometimes you need an approach just for today.

I find that when I'm mentally scattered and without a plan, it's because I have too much energy or too little. I'm a human pinball machine: either poised to bounce between projects and people or completely out of service. Those two extremes tend to push out my ability to **prepare** since I'm too wired or too tired to **notice** and **adjust** with much rationale.

If you've also felt like you are too much for today or today is too much for you, I have two frameworks, both using TODAY as an acronym, that might help you kindly focus on the day in front of you.

When you wake up feeling open and outgoing, with more energy than you know what to do with, focus that outward energy with this framework:

Tricky

Optional

Delightful

Active

Yes

What feels **tricky** today? Is there something in your schedule that has you stumped? You likely have the energy to solve a few logistical problems, so enjoy the process of applying thoughtful attention and a little creativity to whatever is in front of you. Maybe you are Chauffeur Mom during the afternoon, but you also have an early-evening meeting and still haven't figured out how to squeeze in dinner. That's tricky. Figure out the tricky things before they become too complicated and celebrate the fact that you have enough energy to solve tricky problems at all.

What is **optional** today? The more energy you have, the more convinced you are you can do anything. While that's great, it's not necessary. As you make a to-do list or think through your day, name what's optional. Whether you get to it or not is of no consequence.

What is **delightful** today? When you're outwardly focused and feeling productive, it's easy to activate your inner robot: *Must. Complete. Tasks.* Thankfully, delight is your robot fail-safe. What on the docket is delightful? If nothing is, what can you make time for? Even while you're getting a lot done, notice what is joyful, fun, and delightful around you.

What is **active** today? What needs tending to or finishing? Maybe there's a project at work you're wrapping up, or it's

Thursday, which means you clean the bathrooms. You can also notice what's active within you. Are you optimistic? Excited? Focused? Name what is active in and around you.

Now that you've considered these four areas, what are you going to say **yes** to? In other words, **what matters most**? It can be a specific item on your to-do list or something intangible, like a surprising feeling of confidence you want to nurture throughout the day. What are you saying yes to?

Tricky, optional, delightful, active, and **yes.** Consider those for an energetic *today.*

On the flip side, what about the days you wake up and would rather stay in bed? What happens when you don't have much to give and there's no to-do list, strategy, or routine to lean on? Try this.

Tender

Output

Delegate

Accept

Yes

What feels **tender** today? This could be a relationship, the residue of a conversation that's still taking up mental real estate, or even your physical body. You might feel pressure to complete tasks on someone else's timeline or shame that you can't seem to get everything done. No matter what it is, name what's tender.

What is your realistic **output** today? Some days, you just don't have enough gas in the tank, and as much as you're able, honor that. Without any bootstrap or hustle energy, what do you genuinely have the energy for today? Be honest about your output so you can focus your limited energy on the wisest thing.

What can you **delegate** today? When you're low on energy, the default is to wallow in not being able to get your stuff done. Instead, delegate what you can. Hand off tasks to a partner, a kid, a coworker, a professional service, or the fast-food drive-through. Don't sleep on delegating to a future version of yourself that will have more energy than you have today. Delegation isn't lazy or selfish. It's kind.

What do you need to **accept** today? Because you live in a production-driven society, low-energy days often lead to shame because you can't do what you think you should. I don't want that for you. Instead, learn to accept the reality of what's in front of you. Accept that you're in a season of tedium as a caregiver or in a job that you really dislike. Accept that you simply don't have enough to give today. Accept that someone else will load the dishwasher for you and won't do it the way you would, but that you'd rather it be done than be done a certain way.

And finally, in light of today's information, what are you going to say **yes** to? Sure, that can mean an item or two on a to-do list, but it can also mean saying yes to quiet, slowness, idleness, or waiting for tomorrow. It can mean saying yes to yourself and offering kindness and rest as much as your schedule and life allow.

Tender, output, delegate, accept, and **yes.** Consider those for a gentle *today*.

The reason that both TODAYs end in **yes** is that regardless of your energy, schedule, or obligations, you need to name what matters each day. The more you do that, the more wisdom, kindness, and confidence you'll feel in your decisions, despite what your day looks like.

TO RECAP

Fragmentation and urgency are on a quest to slowly break your brain, so approach them with caution each and every day, remembering all the while that you'll likely need different things on different days.

Honor the energy of your varying days by prioritizing what's important and tending to the necessary before it becomes urgent.

Use either of the TODAY acronyms to help you name where you are and what you need, showing yourself tremendous kindness as you adjust based on the energy you have.

The bounds of today hold plenty, and it's beautiful to start where you are.

13. **How to Make a Better To-Do List**

The human brain is unreal—storing information, cataloging sensory input, retrieving the location of your keys, and inexplicably remembering every last lyric of Paula Cole's "I Don't Want to Wait," despite not having heard that song in fifteen years. And it does that while also telling the rest of your organs to keep you alive. Wild.

While our brains are remarkable, the constant fragmentation and manufactured urgency of our modern world have them looking a bit rode hard and put up wet. Not only that, but we often expect our brains to perform in ways they weren't designed to.

For example, multitasking. The brain is not meant to multitask, especially not in the consistent, prolonged way we force it to. As we learned in the last chapter, too much multitasking makes it hard for the brain to stay focused, even when it wants to. That's a shame.

The brain is also not meant to effortlessly remember disparate things, despite its best efforts. That's why lists are great, and I'm sure we both use them all the time. I've always loved them because I love not forgetting things, but these words from Robert Kraft in *Psychology Today* offered surprising clarity on the value of lists:

> Lists are useful because they document what we ordinarily forget. Memory strongly prefers internal structure, and without this structure, remembering is hard work. Unlike stories—in which events are connected by cause and effect—items on a list have no internal structure, except verticality. The first item on a list does not cause the second. A series needs to be written—otherwise, we will forget what's on it.[1]

I find that super illuminating. *Of course* our brains have trouble remembering everything on our to-do list; the tasks have no connection, save being on the same list.

Additionally, there is so much to do, and as you'll recall, women are expected to do more than their fair share, compelling us to pursue "a better way" for getting everything done. Whether externally with new tools or internally with shame spirals, we're constantly evaluating and fixing our lives, even parts that aren't really a problem.

As Celeste Headlee writes in *Do Nothing,* "This drive to leverage every moment eventually gave rise to an obsession with life hacking and a pursuit of ever more complex, arcane, and counterintuitive methods to accomplish what we probably know how to do already."[2]

That stings a little, but it's also hilarious.

So, here we are: a brain full of stuff to remember, calendars packed to the gills, a graveyard of productivity tools, cultural pressure from an unfair system, and the compulsion to hack something we already know how to do.

What's the solution?

Lighten the load.

The Lighten the Load Framework

To-do list frameworks come in all shapes and sizes, and I've tried them all to varying degrees of success or failure. Mostly failure. I've filled notebooks, purchased planners, and downloaded apps to help me keep track of all there is to do. The only thing that has ever stuck is what I'm about to share with you.

I arrived at this idea so intuitively that it's been challenging to articulate, even for this book. It's always been something I've just *done.* Thankfully, I kept trying to put words to it, and now you're reading them! I hope you'll feel excited to use this idea in your own life. At the risk of sounding cocky, I think you will.

Here's the basic idea.

When you have too much to do (which is kind of always), you need a way to manage the chaos. However, ever-changing energy outputs, expectations, and emergencies can change your day on a dime, causing your previously constructed plans to no longer work. In short, women need versatility. We need a system robust enough to hold the fullness of life, nimble enough to handle regular pivots, and thoughtful enough to help us stay grounded.

Lighten the Load does just that.

The Lighten the Load framework has four main steps:

1. Make It Visible: Get it out so you can figure it out.

2. Make It Matter: Assign significance to everything.

3. Make It Smaller: Turn projects and chaos into decisions and actions.

4. Make It Happen: Put everything in its place.

I'll spend this entire chapter breaking down the pieces and parts of this framework, but before we jump in, I'd like to remind you of something very important.

You don't have to do this whole thing.

Four steps is a lot of steps, especially when you have three minutes to get out the door and just need to know what you're supposed to do today. (Go back a chapter for that kind of simplicity, or just make whatever list you want.) The rest of this chapter isn't meant to be a big system you follow without any discernment. Remember, you're bringing your whole self to the table here. How you're wired, what you need, and what is specifically happening in and around you take precedence over following this system to the letter. Promise me you will not follow this system to the letter unless you are genuinely jazzed to do so.

> **How you're wired, what you need, and what is specifically happening in and around you take precedence over following this system to the letter.**

As I explain this framework, notice any particular element that sparkles for you. Even though this system is connected, its pieces can be used individually at any time and in any way you'd like.

In fact, using Lighten the Load is like creating a capsule wardrobe. You can isolate the items in your closet that you're excited about wearing, that make the most sense in the season you're in, and you can see what holes you might want to fill. Some people do that with every single item of clothing, and some do it with just a category, like shoes or sweaters. No matter how in depth you choose to go, thoughtfully curating even one element of your wardrobe in preparation for an upcoming season makes getting dressed that much easier. The same is true of your time.

Going through the framework of Lighten the Load from top to bottom is like creating a capsule to-do list for your season. You'll learn to wisely look at everything in front of you and then thoughtfully decide what you'll actually keep. Much like with a wardrobe, you can declutter and curate everything or prioritize only one area. No matter how much or little you purge, your load will still feel lighter. Once we get to the next chapter, you'll learn how to plan your week and productively "get dressed" with the tasks you've already chosen.

I suggest going through this process no more than once a month. Anything more frequent is likely unnecessary and will waste energy that could be spent on a book, a conversation, a hobby, or a nap. Such a shame.

Are you ready to Lighten the Load? Let's get into it.

1. Make It Visible

Get it out so you can figure it out

My brain is a caffeinated squirrel. She is always hoarding, always frantic, always darting from place to place. My body is more or less normal, but my brain? My brain is a situation.

She is also rather dramatic, assigning equal urgency and value to everything within her. Frankly, she's a bit of a diva. Squirrels always are, right? Consequently, I need to regularly dislodge what's packed tight in my brain, making it **visible,** and my favorite way to do that is with a brain dump.

A brain dump, according to Merriam-Webster, is "the act or an instance of comprehensively and uncritically expressing and recording one's thoughts and ideas (as on a particular topic)."[3] When it comes to our overwhelmed brains, a comprehensive, uncritical practice is a welcome sight.

Thankfully, doing a brain dump is quite simple: Write down everything that's on your mind.

However, I do have a disclaimer.

Just because you can write down everything that's on your mind doesn't mean you should. I used to write down literally everything and taught others to do the same. *Everything* is the "You Are Here" map. *Everything* is hacking things you already know how to do. *Everything* is writing down parts of your life that are actually going fairly well! *Everything* is not the best use of your energy. While you can certainly write down whatever you want, I'd encourage you to be judicious in your brain dump. Too many entries can muck up the process, and life might already feel mucky enough.

Instead of writing down *everything,* write down only what is causing your brain to feel full in the first place, and that usually falls into one of three categories:

1. I'm overwhelmed by it.

2. I don't have a plan for it.

3. I really want to do it.

The projects, tasks, curiosities, and situations that tend to pack your brain to capacity are likely in one of those three categories. As you brain-dump, write down what is overwhelming,

does not yet have a plan, or you really want to do. If something does not fit one of those three categories, let it pass by.

You can make this list by thinking through specific areas of life like home, work, relationships, celebrations, and any number of others. You can also use your calendar as a guide. Much of what we hold in our brains is based on something that is scheduled to happen, and most of that is on your calendar. Or you can just be random. That's my tendency when I'm exceptionally scattered, so if chaos is your baseline, that is perfectly fine.

Just get it out so you can figure it out.

> # Just get it out so you can figure it out.

I've done enough brain dumps to know that some weird things might show up on your list. I once wrote "Should I host Thanksgiving this year?" *in June.* Sweet Kendra. School just got out, baby girl. You are fine. But that's what was on my brain at the time, and it felt overwhelming. Make the weird stuff visible too.

Now listen up. A brain dump is not your to-do list. I repeat: *A brain dump is not your to-do list.* Otherwise, you'll end up planning Thanksgiving at the pool like a weirdo. Stop it right now.

A brain dump is a **decision queue.** It is the holding pen for all the things that could go on your to-do list, making what is overwhelming, necessary, or important **visible.**

> # A brain dump is not your to-do list. A brain dump is a decision queue.

Once you can see what's clogging your brain, it's time to look at the list and figure out what actually matters.

2. Make It Matter

Assign significance to everything

A Lazy Genius is a genius about the things that matter and lazy about the things that don't. If you don't practice naming what matters, by default you'll try to make everything matter. That is one of the many reasons you are so very tired.

Instead of trying to do everything that's now visible, name what is most important. That way you can organize your time according to what matters most. You do that by assigning significance.

You are welcome to look at your brain dump list and assign significance using whatever rubric you like, but I love using the terms *lazy* and *genius* to help me see what I want to prioritize. Genius items get most of my time and energy, while lazy items get whatever happens to be left.

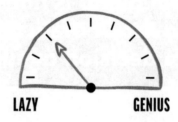

LAZY　　　　　　**GENIUS**

Before we continue, I'd like to say a quick word to my fellow recovering perfectionists. Laziness, especially in this context, is not bad. In fact, part of being a wholehearted, integrated person is embracing that you can't do A-level work in every part of your life. You must actively choose to let some things be easy or lazy so that you can focus on what matters the most. When you think about your season of life, what do you wish was easier? It still needs to happen (meals come to mind), but the energy you have for it is fairly low. This isn't laziness; it's wisdom.

Intentionally send your leftover energy into whatever areas in your current season matter less.

These *lazy* and *genius* labels can work as a binary or on a spectrum. If you'd like to mark items on your brain dump list with either word, go for it. If you'd like to use a number system where *lazy* is a one and *genius* is a ten, do that! If you'd like to use a rainbow set of pens or highlighters, with red signifying the most important and purple the least, color up that list, pal.

I've also used the phrases *make it matter* and *make it easier* to distinguish between these two energies if words are more helpful than colors or numbers.

Essentially, you are naming what gets your best and what gets the rest by **assigning significance** to everything that you're overwhelmed by, don't have a plan for, or really want to do.

Before we move on to the next step, let's pause to consider those things you really want to do. Some things deeply matter to you but do not make as much sense in a particular season. Perhaps you need permission to let go of an expectation, or you need to be realistic about the scope of something that matters.

Let's say one of the things on your brain dump list that you really want to do is to plant a vegetable garden. You've made that desire visible, but then you struggled to assign the right significance. It could be that in your heart, you know there isn't enough time in your current season for a garden, but you're resistant to letting it go.

I get it. I understand how hard it is when something we genuinely want to make happen doesn't quite fit within the boundaries of what matters in the season. Letting those things go sucks, and you're allowed to grieve that loss. As a reminder, at the base of our PLAN Pyramid is what matters most in this season of life, and while that foundation helps us make wise decisions, it doesn't mean those decisions are always easy. Letting go is really hard.

But as you do let go, **notice** why. Sometimes we can **adjust** what matters (see how those PLAN words keep coming up?) to fit into our season and still receive the joy of something we really want to make happen. For example, you're probably letting go of that garden because it's too big. Is there a smaller version you do have time for? Maybe you can choose a favorite vegetable that can grow in a pot instead of a plot, adding "pot a tomato plant" to your brain dump list and putting an all-caps

"GENIUS" next to it. You're more likely to actually do the task because you made it visible, made it matter, and then **made it smaller.** That's next.

3. Make It Smaller

Turn projects and chaos into decisions and actions

You have a visible list of what is overwhelming, what needs a plan, and what you enthusiastically want to make happen. You've assigned significance to those things, naming what matters most during this season so you can know how to distribute your limited energy. These are excellent steps. But even still, you will without question have items that are too big to manage.

You have to make things smaller in order to make them happen. We do that by turning projects and chaos into decisions and actions.

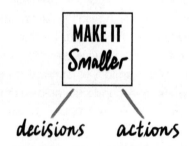

Not everything on your brain dump list needs to be smaller, but it's helpful to have a lens through which to decide if something does. I find that two types of items are always too big: **projects** and **chaos.** Let's start with projects.

Things like "plan our vacation," "finish the garage renovation," and "go Christmas shopping" are too big to check off in one go. Why? They are projects, and projects require many checked boxes to be completed. But because you've listed your project as an individual task, not only will you struggle to actually do it, but you will also always be overwhelmed when you *see* it. Projects must be made smaller, and we'll deep-dive that in chapter 17.

> **Essentially, you make something smaller by breaking it down into decisions and actions:** *What do I need to decide, and what do I need to do?*

The other thing you need to make smaller is chaos. Chaos, whether environmental or mental, is usually caused by some kind of life transition or a prolonged difficult season. When you start a new job while homeschooling your kids and your mother just got diagnosed with Parkinson's, that feels chaotic. That's a life transition pile-on, and you cannot check that off. The same is true of a prolonged season that's run you ragged. You can't write "deal with how I never have enough time" or "figure out how to work from home" as a singular task. That is making chaos more chaotic. We've already talked about how to make chaos smaller by naming what matters, but anytime you need a reminder, revisit chapter 3.

Essentially, you make something smaller by breaking it down into decisions and actions: *What do I need to decide, and what do I need to do?*

As you look at the items on your brain dump list, all marked according to their significance, find the things that are the most important. Do those items still feel overwhelming? Do they need to be made smaller? Maybe something would feel more doable if it was broken down into individual actions and individual decisions.

"Decorate for Christmas" becomes a series of decisions (*When am I going to decorate? Am I going to use a theme or color palette? Am I going to make the kids help me?*) and a series of actions (bring all the bins down from the attic, go shopping for anything extra and fun, rearrange the living room furniture to make room for the tree, decorate the tree, put lights up outside, get the hooks to hang the stockings, and hang the stockings).

Let's pause here because I want to make two observations.

The first is that this is why I love the Lazy Genius principle **decide once.** When you make a decision one time about one thing and then just let it ride until it doesn't work anymore, you remove so much of your mental load. For each of the three Christmas decorating decisions I used as examples above, I made one decision years ago: I decorate the Saturday evening after we get home from our town holiday parade, I use the same decorations every year, and I don't make my kids help me because I'd rather stay happy (but they can help if they want). Done.

As you practice Lighten the Load, notice where you can decide once in order to make repeated projects progressively easier over time.

My second observation is that we forget how many decisions and actions we truly have. I listed seven actions as an example of how to break down "decorate for Christmas," and those seven are just a snippet of the reality. This is why I implore you to be kind to yourself as you make tasks smaller. There are so many things to do and so many things you *are* doing. Acknowledge this so that you can be realistic and compassionate toward yourself when you feel like there's just too much to do.

Because there probably is.

Not only that, but depending on your level of executive functioning, even something like "pay the bills" can feel too big. Be kind and make "pay the bills" smaller by writing down "gather the bills." No item or kindness is ever too small.

Make it visible, make it matter, and then make it smaller. Don't feel like you have to make your entire list smaller at once. Just choose the most significant thing and make it as small as you currently have the energy for. If you can keep going, keep going. Distill your brain dump list into decisions and actions, and be as kind as possible as you do.

Now let's **make it happen.**

4. Make It Happen

Put everything in its place

If you've followed Lighten the Load to this point, you now have a list of decisions and actions that are small enough to do. But your journey isn't over, my friend. You still need to make them *happen.*

Making things happen requires some kind of connective structure. Remember, when it comes to most to-do lists, the first item does not cause the second. The tasks are on the same paper, but there's nothing similar about the urgency, order, or energy required. To make a better to-do list, one that adjusts to the complexities and surprises of your life, you need to know where you are, what you need to do, and what can be let go at any time. You want a to-do list that responds *to you,* not a list you have to respond to.

You want a to-do list where the parts are telling the same story.

To that end, I give you four different ways to organize your decisions and tasks so that you can put them in their proper place.

1. Now, Soon, Later, Never Mind is organized by **urgency.**

2. What's in the Tank is organized by **energy.**

3. All Together Now is organized by **similarity.**

4. Pick One is chosen with **humanity.**

Let's look at all four.

1. Now, Soon, Later, Never Mind

I use this approach the most because my default is to make everything feel urgent. Assigning *appropriate* urgency is one of the kindest things I can do for my caffeinated squirrel brain.

Look at your list of tasks, whether from the full Lighten the Load process or just a random list you made on a Tuesday, and rewrite or label each item with **now, soon, later,** or **never mind.** I prefer to rewrite because it gives me a more ordered, connected to-do list, but you do what works best for you.

Now is self-explanatory. If you don't do it now, things could get hairy. Deciding dinner when it's already six, paying the credit card bill that was due a week ago, or getting the cupcakes you just found out your kid volunteered to bring to school tomorrow. Those are now items.

Soon is relative to your own timing and basically means after now. Don't let the soon things keep you from doing what you need to do first, but they're up next when you've cleared the decks a little.

Later is something that is necessary but definitely not urgent. However, if you continually leave things for later and let them become urgent, you'll constantly feel underwater. Just keep in mind that it's good to tend to the necessary before it becomes urgent.

And finally, **never mind.** You might not have too many of these, but there is always something that has no business taking your brainpower, like planning Thanksgiving in June. I don't even need to put that on the later list. It's so absurd that, for me, it gets a never mind.

However, those out-of-place items often have something to tell you. While unnecessary for your list, they might be illuminating something you need to see.

You know Thanksgiving is currently a never mind item, but it still feels tender. Ask yourself why. What if it's because your judgmental sister-in-law sent you a text the other day about how your Mother's Day gift to her mom didn't fly? Your brain knows that it's your turn to host Thanksgiving this year, and you're already subconsciously stressed out about your sister-in-law's reaction to how well you'll come through. Thanksgiving in June is still a never mind, but it brings up something else that's important, something that needs some tending.

Not every never mind is that heavy, but don't automatically dismiss something until you know why it's on the list in the first place.

I love using these four labels because they are not tied to a particular day or time. Now is relative, allowing you to notice and adjust based on what is happening in and around you. When you don't get to your now items today, you're less likely to feel like a failure if that list isn't labeled today. Today might throw you seven curveballs, making tomorrow feel like you're already behind. Instead, what was now today remains now tomorrow. While that approach can enable some pretty hardcore procrastination, it's still kinder than most to-do lists we make. Be reasonable with what now means and utilize the versatility this approach offers.

> # When your tasks have appropriate urgency, you can put them in a manageable order, empowering you to more calmly and efficiently get things done.

When your tasks have appropriate urgency, you can put them in a manageable order, empowering you to more calmly and efficiently get things done.

2. What's in the Tank

If you can tell your energy is either here to play or here to kick everyone out of the house, you might want to organize your to-do list accordingly.

What's in the Tank allows you to look at what's on your plate and adjust what you'll do based on your energy. As we've already established, being a woman is like being on a hormonal merry-go-round, and it's culturally subversive and beautifully human to honor that movement with specific time-management strategies.

Look at your list of tasks and consider connecting them to the phases of your menstrual cycle or the different types of energy you regularly experience. It's not an exact formula because we're all different human beings, but it works a lot more often than you might think. We discussed the four phases of the menstrual cycle and the types of tasks best suited to them in chapter 9, but here's an overview.

The week or two right after your period (spring) is when you **prepare.** The short window of ovulation (summer) is when you **live.** The long stretch, including PMS, before your period (fall) is when you **adjust.** The time of bleeding (winter) is when you **notice.** I love how it all lines up so beautifully.

Start learning what tasks line up with what energy. For example, you could write "plan our lake day" under **prepare,** "hang out with Sarah" under **live,** "organize hall closet" under **adjust,** and "fill out permission slips" under **notice.**

Obviously, there are certain tasks that can't wait three weeks until you're in your luteal phase, so this approach isn't prescriptive. It's merely a guide to help you see what types of tasks go where and if it's possible to wait until you're better equipped to do them. When it works, it works wonderfully.

3. All Together Now

Charles Darwin said, "A man who dares to waste one hour of time has not yet discovered the value of life,"[4] and I could not disagree with that statement more. Sometimes wasting time *adds* to life's value, especially in Western culture, where efficiency and optimization are the linchpins of everything. Wasting time is not poisonous to your soul.

However, there's nothing wrong with wanting to do things

quickly, as long as you don't try to do *everything* quickly. Slow, idle, quiet things are important and should be pursued. But whenever you'd like to get things done efficiently, try All Together Now. The idea is to combine tasks that have similar requirements and make a plan to do them at the same time.

Categorize your tasks into groups like "returns to drop off," "calls to make," "emails to send," "activities to plan," "paper tasks" (pay bills, fill out permission slips, write a birthday card, etc.), and any other category that surfaces from your broad list of smaller decisions and actions.

I don't know about you, but I tend to procrastinate the administrative stuff. Consequently, it piles up on my to-do list until all the words become visually overwhelming. All I see is a lot to do, not collections of similar tasks that I can batch and quickly get done. If you're the same and you find your eyes bouncing around the decisions and actions not knowing where to begin, try All Together Now.

Grouping similar items together will likely make the list feel more manageable, helping you to complete it that much faster.

4. Pick One

Let's be real here. Some days, you just don't have anything. Organizing a list sounds impossible, and doing any of the tasks on it is like walking through a pool of molasses while wearing a winter coat.

There are days when you simply do not have the capacity to be responsible. Whether it's mental or physical illness, grief, or a brain at maximum capacity, honor your humanity by not forcing yourself to power through. I'm not saying there will never be a time you have to buck up and get something done, but I want you to start with kindness, not productivity or responsibility. Remember, staying grounded is better than staying on task.

When you feel too overwhelmed to make a decision, Pick One. Literally, just pick one thing on your list. Or add a new thing that you know you can do to honor your own humanity, like "take a nap." You are in charge of your list. Your list is not in charge of you.

TO RECAP

The disconnected things on a to-do list might get sporadically checked off, but not without emotional, energetic consequences. Women need a more versatile way to choose what to do and when to do it.

Try Lighten the Load. Take what you're overwhelmed by, what you don't have a plan for, or what you really want to do, and make it visible with a brain dump. From there, make it matter by assigning significance to each task. Next, make it smaller by turning projects and chaos into decisions and actions. Finally, make it happen by putting everything in its place, using some form of categorization (urgency, energy, similarity, or humanity) to connect the tasks with each other.

There are far more ways to make a to-do list than the framework I've shared here. Even though Lighten the Load, whether applied comprehensively or piecemeal, is dependable and versatile, the point is not to just do what I say. The point is for you to recognize that you need different tools at different times, so get comfortable using whatever works best for you.

14. **Plan a Week**

If Lighten the Load is a capsule wardrobe, planning your week is getting dressed.

I love planning my week. I love a rhythm small enough to manage but large enough to rest in. It just feels good. It feels even better when I have thoughtful tools to make it easier:

- The PLAN Pyramid helps me approach my life in a balanced, responsive, integrated way so I don't overcorrect or forget what matters.

- Remembering that I'm a painter helps me focus on the fullness of what I bring to the table instead of just focusing on my tasks.

- Lighten the Load is my to-do list queue, clarifying the decisions and actions that make the most sense for the season I'm in.

Having these tools and perspectives helps me "get dressed" every week, empowering me to choose "outfits" that make the most sense.

I might plan one day with a lot of detail, organizing each hour according to a full schedule and a robust to-do list, and on another day in the same week, I might be content with a couple of tasks on a sticky note and nothing planned.

It's the same as getting dressed. Some days, you go with a full ensemble, complete with multiple layers, jewelry, shoes, and coordinating nail polish. Other days, you throw a comfy sweater over your pajamas and call it good.

Both outfits, as well as everything in between, count. All of it is still *you.* You're simply choosing what to wear according to what you need, and that's how I want you to practice planning a week, too.

But first, let's talk about what might get in the way.

The Sunday Scaries

I know you need to make lists, check off boxes, and do the things grown-ups have to do, and that's never more pressing than at the beginning of a new week.

Which is why we need to talk about the Sunday Scaries.

The Sunday Scaries is the label for the anticipatory stress of a new week—when you see what's coming and legit freak out.

Perhaps you have historically tried to fight that feeling with an intense session of planning. Sunday night comes, and you sit on your couch, surrounded by a new planner, a jar of pens and highlighters to make it look cute, a small stack of cookbooks because you feel like a trash person for making the same meals all the time, and your laptop opened to your newly color-coded Google Calendar because, who knows, maybe the color green is what you've been missing.

This feeling of the Sunday Scaries is ripe for ushering in old patterns. Sunday night is when robot energy hums and "You Are Here" maps get outlined. Sunday night is when you can see your week spread out like a picnic in front of you, and suddenly you feel that call to greatness again. *I really should be doing more,* you think.

So, without considering your season of life, your hormones, your family's energy, or the water heater that's going to bust in two days, you build your machine. You create your puzzle. You plan complicated outfits that all include hard pants both literally and figuratively. You gather your tools and manufacture the week you've been conditioned to pursue.

Chill, baby girl.

> # You're not here to play an intense game of Barbies with your life. You're here to *live it.*

When Sunday night rolls around, take a deep breath. You're not here to play an intense game of Barbies with your life. You're here to *live it.*

Let's talk about how.

How to Lazy Genius Your Week

I want you to feel like your week is in a flow, like you're on an inner tube floating down a lazy river and not on a decrepit raft navigating white water.

Thankfully, we've already started calming the waters by changing the paradigm. You have The PLAN Pyramid to help you see your life, you have the painting analogy to help you see yourself, and you have Lighten the Load to help you see your tasks. You are honoring your very humanity as you focus on **integration** instead of greatness. All of this creates calmer waters, which thrills me to no end, and I hope you're having as much fun as I am.

But how do you get down the lazy river? Or, back to the closet analogy, how do you choose what to wear? In short, how do you practically and tangibly plan a week?

With The Lazy Genius Method.

The Lazy Genius Method is a five-step process that helps you wisely simplify and practically improve just about anything. It's fluid because the steps intuitively connect, it's expansive because it can become as simple or complex as you need it to be, and it's powerful because it can be applied to literally anything.

Knowing we're about to learn another set of steps likely has you either jazzed or freaked out. For the latter folks, I get that, and I don't want to overwhelm you. In fact, if you feel like you are in a great place to pause here and live with what you've already learned, please do that. The PLAN is not a system to follow but a way to *see.* If you feel like seeing anything else right now will blind you, skip to another chapter or come back later.

For those of you who are chomping at the bit for another list of steps, especially a list that will help your week flow better, let's do it.

Here are the five steps of The Lazy Genius Method:

1. Prioritize: name what matters most

2. Essentialize: get rid of what's in the way

3. Organize: put everything in its place

4. Personalize: feel like yourself

5. Systemize: stay in the flow

While you could certainly go through these steps with pen and paper, writing down thoughtful answers and spending a solid amount of time doing it, you can also zip through this method quickly in your head. Just because it's an ordered list doesn't mean it has to be complicated or take a lot of time. Get comfortable with the order, spend time where you want to, and stay loose. This isn't a test. It's just here to help.

Let's walk through each step together.

1. Prioritize

Start by naming what matters most this week.

There are no rules here. Some of you love that, and some of you are mad at me. "No rules? What kind of anarchy is this?!" You'll be okay.

Take a moment to notice how you're feeling in your body, what's coming up in your schedule, what's going on with your family, and what stuff needs to get done. As you compassionately assess where you are, notice what rises to the surface. What matters this week?

A week is long and you are complex, so it's okay to have a few things. I find three priorities to be a solid place to start. Your priorities can be practical, like getting a gift for a friend's birthday, or personal, like remembering that you're allowed to say what you need this week.

Start your weekly plan by naming what matters.

2. Essentialize

I always love these five steps, but depending on the context, certain steps just shine. When it comes to planning a week, **essentialize** is like the daggum sun. Essentializing is making sure you have what you need and you get rid of what's in the way, and there are *so many things in the way of what matters.* You could spend hours essentializing.

I know I sound excited, but please do not do this. Do not spend hours. You don't have them. Instead, when you essentialize, start small.

You don't need to remove every obstacle or equip every area of your life. Frankly, kids are walking obstacles, and if you have them, you probably want to keep them around (most of the time). The temptation is to create a Machine of Life so you can set it and forget it, but that's not how we do things, is it? That's the other guys' energy, not ours.

> ## You don't need to remove every obstacle or equip every area of your life.

Essentializing for the week looks like skipping that complicated recipe on a busy weeknight, rescheduling or canceling that unimportant meeting, or taking a more peaceful route home from work. It's reading in the carpool line instead of paying bills, changing the burned-out lightbulb in the bathroom so you can actually see your face, or planning lunch with a friend who fills you up.

Essentializing is not optimizing your life. It's naming what matters and then noticing what you need to have or remove in order to make what matters happen. Start small.

3. Organize

In both planning and life, this is where you usually start. When things feel wonky, you organize. No closet, calendar, or chore chart is safe. But if you put things in place first, you're organizing what you don't need. Prioritize, essentialize, and *then* organize.

Since organizing your week feels the most like traditional planning, you might feel inclined to use traditional approaches. And you can. However, I have a couple of suggestions to help you put everything in its place and still stay true to the mindset of The PLAN.

First, you can use the imagery of **flags, chairs,** and **bunting.**

Imagine a lush green yard and that you're about to organize your week in there. Start with the **flags,** or whatever is locked: doctor appointments, staff meetings, playgroups, and the like. In whatever form you're making your plan visible, put the flags in their place. Next, move on to **chairs.** Where are you going to metaphorically sit and *not* be productive? Like, *on purpose.* Rest, play, and joy deserve a place every week, if not every day, so make space for them in your plan. Finally, consider **bunting.** I'm kind of obsessed with Webster's definition: "a lightweight loosely woven fabric used chiefly for flags and festive decorations."[1] I like to think of bunting as those things strung between your flags and chairs, contentedly waiting for you whenever you're ready: the YouTube video of birdsong you listen to while doing a part of your job you don't especially love, the laundry waiting to be folded for when your daughter is independently playing, the voice text you'll leave a friend while you drive to the grocery store. Bunting is super chill.

Second, if you're more linear than imaginative (it's me, hi, I'm literal, it's me), you can organize your week by deadlines. Simply place decisions and actions on the days that you'd like to get them done. Start with the ones that matter most, and once those are in place, balance out your week in a reasonable way with whatever is left. I like to write the days of the week on a grid and write my tasks from my Lighten the Load list, or things that just come up, under the day I want to do them. That way,

I'm not looking at one entire list for the week. Instead, I'm making the list smaller and then putting it in a place that makes my stuff more likely to get done.

It feels like half the internet is cat memes and the other half is ways to organize your time. In fact, with the options so plentiful, you might not need much help in this area because you already have a method you love. But now you know to organize *after* you prioritize and essentialize, all while embracing the energy of The PLAN, the goal of integration, and the beauty of today.

List stuff out on paper, block it out digitally, set reminders on your phone, or simply be where you are, trusting that your memory and intuition will keep you on track. Whatever you do, reasonably and compassionately put what matters in its place.

4. Personalize

You want to feel like yourself this week, so what do you need in order to do that? And because you're likely a lady with fluctuating hormones, how can you kindly embrace your specific energy this week?

If you are menstruating and you have three big social events on the calendar, you've got some adjusting to do. How can you feel like yourself? Can you take it easy before and after? Can you move something? Skip something? Three social events in any week is a lot, but during a week where you'd like to hibernate? Ouch. Make sure you feel like yourself.

What if you are in your ovulation phase and feel so deeply yourself, but you have nothing fun scheduled? Text somebody! Go to dinner or drinks or on a walk during your lunch break with a friend!

You can also personalize your week by getting your favorite lunchtime takeout on a particularly busy day, wearing clothes that you love, or playing your favorite music. Or you could do what I do and sit on the porch listening to birds. Even though I am squarely a Weird Bird Woman now, I'm more myself when I listen to birds. It's weird, but if weird is you, be weird.

5. Systemize

Systemizing is less about building precise machinery and more about just keeping things in a flow, and flow is generally characterized by *ease*. Thankfully, there is a Lazy Genius principle that is all about ease, and that is **ask the magic question.**

> # Systemizing is less about building precise machinery and more about just keeping things in a flow.

As you look back over your weekly plan, ask yourself that question: *What can I do now to make something easier later?* Choose something from your plan that is either sticky and stressful or sparkly and exciting. Is there anything you can do or plan now that will help make that thing easier later? What is one thing that might keep your week in a flow? Hate me all you want, but this is why I meal-plan. There is nothing like an unknown dinner to throw off my flow, so knowing what we're going to eat makes the whole week easier. I Magic Question those meals by setting phone alarms to pull meat out of the freezer, chopping the carrots and onions for two meals at once, and writing the meals on a whiteboard so my kids don't ask me every four seconds what's for dinner. Pestering kills my flow big-time.

So now you have planned your week, or your week of "outfits." Some of your days are dressed to the nines, and others don't get out of their pajamas. If I personified my own weekdays, Mondays and Tuesdays wear a blazer and hard pants, Wednesdays wear jeans and a cute sweater, Thursdays wear athleisure, and Fridays are in full-on cozies. It's not good for me to have every day look and feel the same, so I balance out my days with different ratios of tasks and rest, flags and chairs, keeping an eye on whatever can kindly and loosely fill in the gaps.

I realize a lot of this is metaphorical, but I'd rather be imaginative and metaphorical than robotic and exhausted. Add some ease into planning your week, pal. You're doing great.

TO RECAP

Planning your week is life-giving and fun when you have the right tools.

Instead of being overwhelmed by the Sunday Scaries, utilize the tools from this book that have resonated with you so far, and plan your week in a compassionate, helpful way.

If you're up for it, go in the right order by following The Lazy Genius Method: prioritize, essentialize, organize, personalize, and systemize.

In a culture that loves a series of checkboxes aimed at reverse engineering an optimized, ideal future, hold fast to The PLAN Pyramid. Everything rests on what matters during this season of your life, on honoring exactly where you are. And as you prepare, adjust, and notice in equal measure, you'll be able to live your life, week by week, day by day, moment by human moment.

And if you just want to take a deep breath and roll into

Monday without a single plan, I'm here for that, too. Remember, staying grounded is better than staying on task, and learning to pivot is more important than learning to plan. You don't have to have a color-coded planner to feel connected to your life.

15. **Plan a Month**

I think every month has a personality.

October is our best friend's cool older sister. March is an introvert who spends all her free time at the library. July is our opinionated aunt who's sunburned and a little drunk. January is an eager CrossFit trainer. May is a loud room mom. February is a bored teenager. December is an oversugared toddler at a bouncy-house birthday party who lost her shoes an hour ago.

Even though our lives often feel repetitious, each month does bring its own vibe, influencing the list of what we need and want to do. When we enter a new month, sometimes we feel excited about the vibe, and other times we want to throw away our planner and hide.

No matter your response, consider starting each new month where you are.

The path of planning a month is different from Lighten the Load in that it specifically incorporates who you are and how you're experiencing your life, not just what you have to do. When you get to the part about putting things for the month in place, pull out your last Lighten the Load list in case it helps you manage your time with more clarity.

Now let's plan a month.

Look Back Before You Look Ahead

Reflection is simply noticing what's already happened on purpose. It's paying attention to the past so you can adjust as you move forward, prepare for the right thing, and intentionally live where you are.

Emily P. Freeman, author, podcaster, spiritual director, and my dearest friend for almost twenty years, is my favorite teacher of this practice. She has modeled and taught how we must look back before we look ahead, so if you want more words about reflection, discernment, and decision-making, look her up.

> # Reflection is simply noticing what's already happened on purpose.

Don't look me up. This is not my strong suit. In fact, noticing my past is so incongruent with how I'm wired that I have to actively choose to reflect. I must plan it into my life, and I *do,* because if I don't reflect first, I plow ahead, reinvent wheels, and try to use ones that broke a long time ago. Not ideal. Adding a reflective rhythm to my life every month has been valuable, and I think it will be the same for you.

Monthly reflection helps you cultivate kindness for your current season of life and empowers you to make wise decisions that support what matters to you.

So, look back at the past month and ask yourself a few questions. Emily has a set of ten that are excellent, and I'll share my favorite three here.[1]

1. What worked and what didn't work?

2. What filled me up and what emptied me out?

3. What's one thing I know for sure moving forward?

These questions help you notice what is easily overlooked so that you can comprehensively and compassionately look ahead. Answer them if you think they'll help you see your upcoming month a little more clearly.

Name What Matters

After looking back, look at where you are now. Consider your schedule and your most recent practice to Lighten the Load. Notice how your calendar is lining up with your menstrual cycle if that matters to you. Be curious about the energy of this upcoming month. Think about your people. Name things you might need.

From that information, name what matters most this month. It's okay if it changes, and it's even okay if you don't follow through. The practice alone is wonderful to build on.

As you name what matters most, categories might be helpful. You might consider specific areas like home, work, relationships, and health. I sometimes feel overwhelmed by too many categories and stick to one or two general ideas, so if that's you too, no worries. Choose what works for you.

I'd also encourage you to pay attention to your body as you name what matters. When you choose something, what do you experience physically? Is your energy calmed or heightened? Is there something about the upcoming month that's causing you noticeable anxiety? Listen to your body in case it's trying to tell you something that you've been too busy to hear. Your body is wise.

> # Listen to your body in case it's trying to tell you something that you've been too busy to hear.

If you feel pressure to get what matters "right," let that go. This is not your only opportunity to examine your priorities, and you'll likely adjust anyway. We just went through the rhythm of planning your week, which includes naming what matters on a regular basis. You can and will adjust as necessary. Remember the equanimity of The PLAN Pyramid. Adjusting is a vital part of living well, so do it just as much as you prepare.

Name Your Have-Tos

Some stuff you just have to do. Procrastinate all you want, but eventually you'll have no choice but to do things like pay bills, buy groceries, wash clothes, go to the doctor, finish the project, and on and on. If something is not already a habit or a routine, write it down in your monthly plan so it's more likely to get done. Since many have-tos are recurring, you might appreciate having a master list of monthly tasks to reference.

Other have-tos happen at infrequent intervals or are singular and circumstantial, things like renewing a car registration, scheduling a mammogram, or buying your kid a Hawaiian shirt for a school band performance even though you know he'll never wear it again. Most months have tasks like this, so if you know something is on the horizon, whether it surfaces during this process or earlier during a Lighten the Load, add it to your have-to list for this month.

Now, not all have-tos are boring or weird or put upon you by someone else. I think fun and rest are have-tos just as much as paying your electric bill is. Prioritize taking care of your body, soul, creativity, and relationships. Typically, we leave those for last, for whatever time is left once all the responsible things are done. I don't need to tell you that strategy is trash, right? Tending to yourself is a have-to.

I do want you to notice one important distinction as you make your list: *Have to* is different from *should do.*

The two certainly overlap, but have-tos feel more polite than should-dos. Have-tos are neutral; should-dos are shameful. I'm not saying the word *should* is inherently bad. It very much is not. But if you hear a voice in your head saying that you *should* be exercising more or you *should* be cooking more homemade meals or you *should* be taking more responsibility at that organization even though you're already stretched thin, be discerning about how much power you give that voice. In many cases, it'll only compel you to do more, and doing more for its own sake is what makes you tired.

> # Doing more for its own sake is what makes you tired.

Be vigilant about what is truly a have-to as you make your list for the month.

Name Your Hope-Tos

What do you hope to do this month? This list is meant to capture things that often get pushed out by the have-tos.

Here is my personal hope-to list this month:

- Find a new pair of black jeans

- Paint a few more spreads in my sketchbook

- Hang out with my friend Haven

- Get drinks with the girls

- Pack away my cold-weather clothes

- Bake something new

- Get three weeks ahead on the podcast

If none of these happen this month, I'll be okay. Sure, I'll wish I had black jeans I love, but I have other nonblack jeans that work fine. I'd love to hang out with Haven since we've both been extra busy lately, but if we don't, we can still text and use Voxer and hug each other at church. I'd love to pack away my cold-weather clothes, but if I don't, my closet will just stay full. I'd love to get three weeks ahead on the podcast, but if I don't, I still have enough time to stay current.

Your hope-to list matters, and I want the things on it to happen for you! Just kindly remember that if they don't, you didn't do anything wrong. You can try again next month, keeping them as hope-tos or moving some to have-tos if there's been a change in status.

Put Everything in Its Place

Let's start with the have-tos, the flags for your month, or whatever needs to happen now.

We start there not because obligation is more important than hope, but because scheduling what is urgent and important at the start of the month, instead of reacting to things as they come, theoretically leaves more time to get your stuff done.

If necessary tasks aren't penciled in, they all sit around until the end of the month, becoming urgent at the same time. And urgency breeds urgency. Now everything is figuratively on fire, and that is a tough environment to reclaim. This is why you spend a few minutes penciling your have-tos into your schedule. You're creating margin and intention around the things that matter before they become an emergency. This way, nothing sneaks up on you, and you have ample room for your hope-tos to actually happen.

So grab your two lists and put the tasks in their place on your calendar or on a list you already check.

Plan to pay bills while waiting in Tuesday's pickup line. Schedule a Saturday night dinner with friends even if you don't know who you'll go with yet. Carve out an hour one afternoon to think through Christmas gifts this year. Put the tasks in place.

If you have a dated planner, especially one with a weekly spread, write your have-tos and hope-tos in the most appropriate week, and when you open your planner to that week, you'll already have tasks patiently waiting for you. For flexible tasks, I like to use tiny sticky notes I can move around.

Just because I plan my month on paper doesn't mean you have to. If you use a list app, transfer anything you just wrote down to it. Also, many apps come with list templates, so consider using one to create your list of recurring have-tos so you don't forget them.

TO RECAP

Every month is different, as is every week within it, so avoid trying to "normalize" a month. Look back at what did and didn't work before, name what matters now, list your have-tos and hope-tos or reference your last Lighten the Load, and put everything in its place.

As you practice naming what matters and noticing and adjusting along the way, your monthly rhythm will find its footing, and you'll feel increasingly connected to your life and to yourself.

16. **Plan a Season**

Let's talk about the seasons.

The Earth offers her fair share: spring, summer, fall, and winter. We have numerous cultural traditions: religious and national holidays, liturgical calendars, and the civic rhythms of school years and election cycles. We encounter multiple life stages, some that are predictable and others that sneak up on us, everything from new jobs and soccer seasons to illness and learning to live after a divorce. There are seasons of rehabbing a broken shoulder, looking for a place to live, grieving a hard breakup, or tightening the budget after an unexpected expense.

Life is a series of seasons, usually several at once, and learning to be present within them will transform your life. That's why what matters *in your current season* is the base of our PLAN Pyramid. So, whether you are entering a new season or need relief from the current one, this process will help you notice where you are, prepare for what you need, adjust with more ease, and live with more contentment.

Acknowledge Where You Are

Your season affects everything, so you need to first acknowledge where you are. Currently, I'm in several overlapping seasons: the kids are home because it's summer, our bathroom is under renovation, I'm writing this book, and I'm a woman in her early forties dealing with my changing body. Because I am in close relationship with various people, their seasons affect me too. My mom just went through a divorce. My church just went through a crisis. My friend just went through an acute loss. When it's all listed out like that, it might feel overwhelming. But I always find that when I take the time to name my specific season, I have so much more compassion for myself. *Good gracious, Kendra, of course you're tired! That's a lot to deal with!*

Acknowledging where I am helps me see the reality of what I need, what I'm capable of, and what I can release. It's a wise reminder of how I can be mindful of my situation and remain kind to myself.

So, as you plan, begin by naming the season you're currently in. It seems obvious, but it's vital.

Look Back and Ahead

Similar to when we plan a month, we plan a season by looking back before we look ahead, and we'll do that by asking a few questions.

Many of them have the phrase *last season,* and that can mean a couple of things. It can mean the previous chronological season—that is, the time just before now—or it can mean the same season from the year before. For example, if you're planning the upcoming summer season, you'll want to look back at last summer, not the most recent spring. Make sense?

Determine what the most appropriate definition of *last season* is for you.

If nothing comes to mind for a particular question, don't fret. Not every question will have a shiny answer, so roll on past if you need to. Write your answers down in a notebook, and don't feel like you need to spend a ton of time here. Just five to ten minutes quickly thinking and jotting down answers will help point you in a direction that honors the season you're in.

Questions for Looking Back

1. **What do I remember from last season?**
   Big, small, funny, sad . . . there are no wrong answers. Simply ask. My memories usually surprise me.

2. **What do my people remember from last season?**
   Different moments resonate with different people, so be sure to ask your friends and family what they remember, too.

3. **What has changed since last season?**
   A million things might be different now than they were before—people, circumstances, geography, family units— and it's helpful to name them.

> **If something significant has changed, your expectations probably should too.**

We often try to cram our current season into the shape of a previous one, and that leads to unmet expectations and disappointment. If something significant has changed, your expectations probably should too.

If this is a brand-new season for you, nothing has changed because you've never been here before, but this is the perfect time to take note that *you've never been here before.* Be kind, please.

4. **What mattered last season that doesn't matter now?**
   The reason to constantly ask what matters is that *what matters will regularly change,* and if it does so without your acknowledgment, a season can feel unsettled. It doesn't make sense anymore, even though it used to. This answer will help identify why.

5. **What was *not* my favorite thing last season?**
   Answering this doesn't make you a Debbie Downer. The purpose, instead, is twofold: It shows you what you'd rather not repeat, and it identifies if a significant disappointment or loss from last season is affecting how you view this one. There's a reason Bessel van der Kolk's book *The Body Keeps the Score* has sold well over two million copies since its 2014 release and continues to live on the *New York Times* bestseller list even now. Our bodies absolutely remember hard things from previous seasons that we haven't intellectualized yet. If there is something keeping you at arm's length from an upcoming season, consider what happened in the last one that might be causing some residual stress or sadness.

   The answer also doesn't have to be heavy. Maybe you didn't love going to that indoor water park last summer, so you're not going back. Case closed.

6. **What made last season satisfying, enjoyable, or fun?**

   You might find that your answer to this question is similar to your answer to the first question: *What do you remember?* That's fine! If a memory stands out *and* it was full of joy and fun, that's an experience worth reflecting on and maybe even trying to repeat.

   Some seasons have fun built in, but that's certainly not true for every season. If you're coming out of one that involved caring for an aging parent or going through grief or being at a job you hate while waiting for another one to work out, you might struggle to name what made that time satisfying, enjoyable, or fun. But I hope you try anyway.

   Remember, good is here now, and the more we look for it, the more often we see it.

7. **What worked well last season and what didn't?**

   This final question is the most practical and will help you know where to focus your energy in this upcoming season. What worked and what didn't? A simple question with illuminating answers.

   Now that you've looked back, let's *look ahead* to your next season.

Questions for Looking Ahead

1. **What would I love to repeat?**

   This could be a trip, a House Rule,* or a party you threw. Literally anything is game. Nothing is too big or small.

---

*Set house rules** is one of the thirteen Lazy Genius principles, and its purpose is to prioritize what matters most in your home with boundaries that everyone living there (hopefully) follows.

2. **What am I excited about?**

    Tap into that excitement now. Prioritize what sparkles. If you're excited about it, that probably means it matters.

3. **What am I already dreading?**

    Every season brings its challenges, and there is likely something about this upcoming season that you're already *over.* Name it here so you can create a way to bring it into the current season more gently.

4. **What are my top three hope-tos for this upcoming season?**

    These are things that feel important and exciting on some level, but you haven't yet locked them in as a sure thing. Name them here so you can prioritize them.

5. **What sights, sounds, smells, and flavors do I love about this season?**

    I did a podcast episode in May 2023 and presented this question as a way to think about summer. Someone sent a message a couple of weeks later to tell me she hadn't thought about seasonal senses before but had named how much she loved the smell and sound of food on the grill. Guess what that led to? Less planning and more pleasure around cooking dinner since she prioritized cooking on the grill.

    This is a sleeper question and can make a huge difference.

6. **What will I be so glad I did or didn't do this season?**

    Remember, you can't make everything matter, and some things are important to let go. Name what you'll be glad you didn't do, prioritize, or worry about.

    Conversely, name what you will be so glad you did when

you look back on this season. It could be a singular experience or a general choice to not worry about what people think of you in a swimsuit.

7. **What needs to be made smaller?**
   You know the importance of this one by now, right? Big projects, tasks, or commitments don't get done by staying big. You have to make them smaller.

In a moment, you'll take a few action steps from the answers to these questions, so there's no need to aggressively break down the big things now. Just note what you're hoping to do that is currently too big to approach.

How to Organize Your Season

At this point, you have a treasure trove of information to move into your next season. What do you do with it all?

You're going to briefly walk through The Lazy Genius Method, particularly the first three steps: prioritize, essentialize, and organize.

1. Prioritize: Name What Matters Most

As you look at the answers to your questions, notice what sticks out. What feels important enough to get top priority in this upcoming season?

As a heads-up, what matters most during your season will occasionally conflict with what matters during a random week within that season, and that's okay. When your immediate needs supersede the seasonal ones, remember that adjusting doesn't make you undisciplined. I think it makes you wise. Simply name an intention.

2. Essentialize: Have What You Need and Get Rid of What's in the Way

Sadly, most of what you've written down or thought about won't happen without some kind of effort, so let's make that process as kind and efficient as possible.

For some people, this is a time to shine. You might love breaking big things into small pieces and extrapolating action steps from random ideas. If that's you, frankly, you need no instruction for this part. Go forth and make your list. You were made for this.

In fact, this would be a great time to take the answers to these seasonal questions on a walk-through of Lighten the Load. Now that you know what matters for the season, you can more easily figure out what to do, what you need, and what to let go.

For other people, this kind of executive functioning is too much, as we discussed in chapter 10. If that's you, I want you to utilize two things as you look at your season: a timer and tiny steps.

When you're feeling overwhelmed by a giant task, like planning a vacation, you assume that task will take forever, and forever is a *really* long time. Sometimes it's easier to quit than keep going, especially when the road is paved with too many choices.

I'm a big fan of thoughtfully thinking about your season, but if some of these ideas just feel like one more thing to complete, start small. Choose one big task from your list, set a timer for five minutes or however long you have the energy for, and write down small decisions and tasks that are part of that big task until you hear a ding. If you still feel okay and want another round, set the timer again.

Let's say you wrote down "go to the beach this summer," but it's already April and you haven't done a thing. While your timer runs, your job is to make that one task much smaller.

You could write "find a place to stay," but do you know what beach you want to go to? If not, write "choose the beach I want to visit." If that's still too big because you don't know how to choose, make that smaller, too. Write "ask Marianne what her favorite beach is."

Nothing is ever too small. Just ask Marianne, and that step, like every other tiny one, moves you toward something that matters.

3. Organize: Put Everything in Its Place

Do this any way you like, maybe even using some part of the Lighten the Load framework from chapter 13, but here are some suggestions for where to "put" each action step for your upcoming season.

- **Write it on the calendar.**
  If it can be scheduled, schedule it.

- **Integrate it into an existing routine.**
  Let's say you light a candle every morning when you make your coffee, and you just named peppermint as one of your favorite scents of the winter. Change out your morning candle to a peppermint one, and you have something that matters without creating any extra work.

- **Give it to someone else.**
  Some things need to be delegated or handed off to someone who is better at them or more excited about them. Or simply someone who isn't you.

- **Create a seasonal ceremony for it.**
  I love opening and closing ceremonies to mark seasons. Sometimes the pieces and parts of an upcoming season can be gathered into one experience that marks the beginning or the end of where you are.

- **Make it into a project.**
  That's the next chapter.

TO RECAP

As you plan a new season, actually PLAN.

Name where you are and what matters now, and rely on that as your foundation for everything. Notice where you are by looking back on what's been, adjust according to what's ahead, and prepare by identifying what's most important and putting it into place.

Hold your plan for the season kindly and loosely, and just be where you are.

17. **Plan a Project**

In the suspense novel *Two Nights in Lisbon* (not your typical source for time-management advice) lies this gem of a quote: "There's always a large category of noncritical projects that can persist for long periods in the nonspecific future, awaiting attention."[1]

That'll preach.

Noncritical projects in the nonspecific future are, next to low-rise jeans and three-way stops, the bane of human existence. They need a plan to happen, so let's make one.

What Makes a Project

In my experience, a project needs four characteristics to be considered a project:

1. It has one primary objective.

2. It has an end.

3. It's out of your ordinary.

4. It requires more than one decision or task.

Let's look at some examples.

Cleaning out the closet is a project. Your primary objective is to get out what you don't need and make the rest look decent; it's over when the closet is organized; it's not in your ordinary routine, like packing your lunch or taking the dog for a walk; and it involves a *lot* of decisions and tasks.

Setting a goal to run a 5K is a project. Your primary objective is to finish the race, and the project is over when that happens. Training for a 5K is likely out of your ordinary, and it requires multiple runs or multiple actions.

One more.

Shopping for holiday gifts is a project. The primary object is to get gifts for everyone that you care about, and the project is over when all the gifts have been purchased.* It's definitely out of your ordinary, often indicated by a mad dash to the mall on December 23, and it requires so many actions and decisions that it might make you cry.

I share these examples so you can see how many projects you have in your life. Trips, home improvements, goals, dreams, chores . . . they're all just projects. And I think you struggle to make progress on them because of those last two characteristics: They're out of your ordinary, and they require a lot of action or decision-making.

That means you need a plan.

Now, you can have unfinished projects. A whole slew of them, in fact. I pass no judgment on anyone living with non-critical projects in the nonspecific future. But if unfinished projects are causing you stress, let's change that.

The reason unfinished projects often cause stress is that

---

*Wrapping gifts is its own project. Even the projects have projects!

they're not done. That's a bit obvious, but it's also clarifying. A project is supposed to have an end, and when that end is in the nonspecific future, you feel like it will *never* be done. Now you're in a pit of despair and start a different project to take the sting off.

Let's try a different process.

How to Finish an Existing Project

If you're over there chilling with literally no open-ended projects in your life, I'd like to respectfully and lovingly call you a liar. Let's figure out how to finish the unfinished.

1. Make a Plan to Assess the Project

Literally write "assess X project" on your to-do list. You need to make time to even think about it, let alone do it. Start small.

2. Assess the Objective

The objective isn't just the practical part. In other words, it's not just "retile the bathroom floor." *Why* do you want to retile the bathroom floor? If you had an antsy, discontent day where you suddenly hated everything about your house and reacted by buying a giant bag of grout and ever since you've been stepping over a giant bag of grout, maybe the project isn't what you need.

When revisiting a project, always consider the original objective. What was the purpose, and has that purpose changed? If the objective no longer matters, congratulations, you can stop reading and just quit the project. You don't have to retile the bathroom after all.

> # When revisiting a project, always consider the original objective. What was the purpose, and has that purpose changed?

If the objective still matters, whether it's different now or still the same, go through the rest of the steps with the correct objective in mind. Otherwise, you'll do the wrong things out of order.

3. Confirm the End Date

Remember, a project is easier to complete when there's an end date involved, whether it's someone else's or your own.

If there is no end date, make an arbitrary one. A deadline will eliminate that nonspecific future. If an arbitrary deadline feels imaginary and doesn't carry weight for you, add some kind of incentive or motivation to it. Make May 6 your arbitrary end date to refinish your dining room table, and invite friends over for a dinner party on May 7. That might give you the motivation to finish something that matters.

Also, be flexible if the end date *needs* to change. Let's say you were going to run a race on a certain date, but you twisted your ankle a month into training. A lot of people, instead of *moving* the end date to allow for recovery, slowly grow frustrated and resentful because they can't get back to normal fast enough. Grieve the change, sign up for a different race, and move the end date. That feels a lot kinder.

4. Set Aside Time for the Project

Have you ever heard of Parkinson's law? It says that work expands to fill all the available time, which is why your regular activities feel like they take up your whole life. Therefore, you must claim and set aside time for your project. You can't just hope to fit it in, because your regular activities will squeeze it out.

For example, I had to set aside time for this book. You might think writing a book is part of my job, and it is in theory. But really, this book is a project. Since my regular work already expands to fill my work hours, I can't expect to write an entire book without setting aside specific project time. As my baseline, I scheduled three long weekends over six months, and I blocked off every Thursday morning as "Book Day." As I got closer to my deadline and had more to get done than the time to do it, I set aside a Saturday morning here, a quick overnight at a hotel there, I worked late when necessary (it's 12:16 A.M. right now), and I got it done.

You can't fit a project into your ordinary life without setting aside specific time. Frankly, I wish I was wrong about that, and I *never* wish I was wrong. We can't get around this one. Set aside time for your project.

5. Break Down the Decisions and Actions

A project is way too big to put on a to-do list, so it's vital to make it smaller. My favorite way to do that is by doing something already familiar in these pages: breaking the project into decisions and actions. Honestly, this is why most of us hate projects. Decisions and actions, especially a lot of them, are kind of a pain.

But if you want to finish a project because the objective matters more than your motivation, you've got to break it down into manageable pieces.

Name every small thing you'll need to do. Name every small thing you'll need to decide. You can separate the two if it helps, or you can keep them all together and sort them chronologically. Do whichever you prefer.

If you want to understand how to best use the time you've set aside and how to reach your objective by the end date, you need to see all the tiny pieces, not just the broad strokes, of your project. But since the decision fatigue of a project will break us all, you can't stop here. In fact, this is where most projects go to die, so the next step is your secret weapon.

6. Schedule the Next Couple of Things

Don't schedule everything, but don't leave everything floating either. Schedule just a couple of things to get a little momentum.

If you've only started thinking about retiling the bathroom, don't feel compelled to immediately schedule the long weekend to complete the project. It's enough to schedule time to watch the instructional videos on YouTube and pick out tile. Once those tasks are done, you can schedule the next couple of things and so on.

7. Keep Checking In

Hopefully you're not the only person doing this project, but if you are, you're your only accountability. Keep checking in on your progress. If someone else is part of this project with you, share the load and take turns checking in on how things are going, delegating and scheduling tasks as needed.

A great time to do this is when you plan for the week or, if the project is big enough, when you plan for the month. Check in with the pieces and parts you broke down and pick the next couple of tasks to do. Make sure you've set aside appropriate time for those things and then put them on the calendar.

If at any point you notice that the project feels off, go back to your objective and your end date—those are likely the culprits—and adjust if you need to.

How to Start a New Project

The process above still matters and still tracks, but if you're considering whether to add a new project to your life, here are some questions to answer first.

1. How will the result of this project affect my life?

2. Do my expectations of the result match the energy I'm willing to give?

3. What will my life look like if I don't do this project?

4. Is there another season when this project makes more sense?

5. Is there something else I can do now that offers a similar result with less time and effort?

6. What will I have to give up in order to do this project now, and is that trade-off worth it?

7. What information do I still need to make a wise decision?

The first four questions have fairly simple answers. If you get as far as the fifth and have been honest with yourself, you might notice that instead of needing to plan a kitchen remodel, you simply have Big Black Trash Bag Energy and just need to put some dishes away. Go do that.

If you get as far as answering the sixth question, you're ready to test how much this project matters, since something else will have to give a little. If you're not willing to think about the reality of what you'll need to let go, it might not be the best time to commit to the project. Right now, you're calm and motivated. Spoiler: That will not always be the case.

I like the seventh question because it leaves space for wisdom. Take a beat, think about it, and notice what else you might be missing.

When you take a few minutes to walk through this process, you'll find not only that projects get done more quickly but that you're doing projects that truly matter to you.

A Final Pro Tip

These questions obviously make sense for bigger projects like home renovations or planning a summer cross-country road trip, but they also work as a trip wire when you get the itch to start cleaning out your entire kitchen. Do you know the end date of that project? Today. That end date is today. Under no circumstances will you be happy with plates and pans on every surface while your enthusiasm fizzled out four cabinets ago. Please don't live in a house full of piles.

If you feel that Big Black Trash Bag itch, ask the new project questions, and see if the answers scratch it.

TO RECAP

Projects have a primary objective and an end date, they are out of the ordinary, and they require more than one decision or action. It's no surprise they often remain undone.

Instead of leaving projects to wither and die while you

exist in a shame spiral, go through this process of assess-
ment, and make a helpful plan. Sometimes you'll discover
the project didn't matter as much as you thought in the
first place, and sometimes you'll get a little momentum.
Either way, remember what matters most in the season
you're currently in.

18. **What to Do with Goals and Dreams**

I have a wonky relationship with goals, and there are two primary reasons.

One, I'm a recovering perfectionist, and I've spent most of my life thinking that not meeting a goal was a failure of devastating proportions. Even though I now intellectually understand how incorrect that is, the message still runs deep enough that I can't set goals without feeling weird. Que será, será.

Two, most of the goals I set over the years had to do with my body. Lose ten pounds, fit into a size whatever, have a flat stomach . . . all thanks to the garbage that is diet culture. I have since changed my tune, preferring to spend my time and energy *living my life* rather than obsessing over my body's size. Even so, every time I set a goal that has nothing to do with my body, I still *think* about my body. Goals and my body are mercilessly intertwined, and I could not be more annoyed about this.

Consequently, I've had to find another way to see goals or else I'd suffocate in my own dysfunction.

So, I created The Someday List.

The Someday List

The Someday List is exactly what it sounds like. It's full of things you'd like to do someday.

"Kendra, is this like a bucket list?" I suppose. The overlap is there. However, a bucket list feels like too much pressure. *Do this thing before you kick the bucket, Kendra, because we're all going to die.* That's true, but it's also kind of intense. The Someday List feels looser, softer. I prefer it, but you name your list whatever you want.

On The Someday List, checking a box is not the end game. That's reserved for projects, and when you feel like it's time to move something from The Someday List to a project, you have the process from the previous chapter to do it.

Until then, you're not weighed down by your "goals." In fact, The Someday List is as light as a feather.

Your Someday List can be full of whatever you like. Grand is not the measurement. Only someday is.

Since you could add all kinds of things to your Someday List, it might be hard to conceptualize, so let's look at mine as an example. I'll show you the list and explain how I check in with it, slowly moving Somedays into projects.

Here is what's on my Someday List:

- Take a family trip to New York City

- Take a do-over trip to New York City with Jamie when she isn't dying*

---

*When my friend and podcast host Jamie B. Golden and I went to New York, she got pneumonia and an ear infection and was mostly dead. I walked around the city alone during the day, and then we ordered takeout and watched movies in the hotel room at night. It was weirdly one of my favorite trips ever because New York plus Jamie in any way is fantastic, but I'd like to try it again when she doesn't have the hospital on speed dial.

- Go to New Zealand

- Learn to play the drums

- Own a vacation home by the water

- See Sara Bareilles in a Broadway show

- Take a long road trip with the family to some national parks

- Have a huge birthday party

- Go back to London

- See Jacob Collier in concert

- Paint something I like enough to hang in my house

That's my list! It's slightly random and totally awesome. But please remember a very crucial detail: **Just because all these things are on the same list doesn't mean I can treat them all the same way.**

> # The achievability of a list rises to the level of the hardest thing on it.

This is our biggest misstep with lists in general. Just because things are written one after the other doesn't mean they're connected or will require the same level of commitment, energy, or decision-making from you. They were just written at the same time.

Additionally, I've always found that the achievability of a list rises to the level of the hardest thing on it. When a challenging thing sits next to an accessible thing, both feel strangely impossible, and that's why you need to categorize.

Because there are infinite categories for your Someday List, let's just start with two that are probably common for most people: trips and skills.

How to Plan a Trip

Of the eleven things on my list, five of them are specific trips. (Two of them will likely *require* a trip, but that's a different energy.)

My five trips are New York City with my family, New York City with a friend, New Zealand, London, and a long family road trip. How does a trip from The Someday List become a project?

Slowly, and one at a time.

If I turn all these trips into projects at once, I'll never go anywhere. Literally. So which trip do I plan *first*?

This is the order for figuring that out:

1. **Choose your preferred time.** Decide in general when you'd like to take each trip. Some might require your kids to be a certain age, or you might want to do something before your parents' mobility becomes an issue. Add a loose sense of timing to each trip as wide as it needs to be. For example, the preferred timing for our family New York trip is between 2024 and 2028.

2. **Organize chronologically.** A trip that you need to take in two years or it won't happen likely takes precedence over one that could happen in five. Organizing chronologically also shows you which trips are less important by allowing you to see how long you have to wait for them.

3. **Roughly determine the expense.** Decide approximately how much money you'll need for the soonest trip. If you have no idea, check transportation and lodging, since those cost the most. If the soonest trip doesn't cost as much as you thought and you can financially manage two trips, figure out the expense for the next one, too. Now do the math of how much you need to put aside a month for your soonest trip(s), and make a note on your to-do list to set that up.

4. **Schedule your trip.** Put the soonest trip on the calendar. Feel free to be random and just block off the days. Even if you change the particular dates (which is likely), space is held. That's what matters. Do this with more than one trip if you want, especially since you have your preferred chronology ready to go.

5. **Make it a project.** Your soonest trip is now a project. Follow the project process to break it down further so you can fold that out-of-the-ordinary planning into your ordinary routine.

Listen, you can be spontaneous and just take a trip. It doesn't have to be super involved. But unless you have a streak of spontaneity in you, you probably won't just hop on a plane with your family and go to Brazil. Most trips require at least a little bit of planning, and this is a great way to do that.

How to Learn or Develop a Skill

The other likely category on your Someday List is skills. These are things you'd like to learn how to do or learn how to do better. I have two: learn to play the drums (a new skill) and learn to paint something I like enough to hang in my house (a develop-ing skill).

Skills are different from trips because there are no end dates. In fact, a skill is hard to translate into a project since the very nature of developing a skill is the development itself. You never really arrive.

That said, if you want to learn or develop a skill, you have to start by moving the skill off your Someday List. You can do that with three questions:

1. Is there a goal?

2. Is there a next step?

3. Am I ready to take that next step?

1. Is There a Goal?

For certain skills, there is a tangible goal, like brushing up on your cello skills so you can play Bach's Cello Suite No. 1 again.

For other skills, like my learning to play the drums, the goal is harder to define. Do I want to be able to play a specific song? Not really. Do I want to be able to play with a band? I mean, it'd be rad, but it's not necessary. Is there a certain technique I want to learn? I don't even know what the techniques are. So other than "learn to play the drums," *which literally could not be vaguer,* I don't have a specific goal.

No worries. Not every skill does.

2. Is There a Next Step?

Whether you have a goal or not, see if there's a next step.

For brushing up on the cello, the next step could be getting your high school cello the next time you visit your parents' house. For my learning to play the drums, it might be doing a little research on where to take lessons.

Keep it small so you'll actually do it.

3. Am I Ready to Take That Next Step?

This answer likely involves multiple factors.

Are you energetically or motivationally ready? Is this a wise season of life to learn this skill? Do you have the resources right now to buy the supplies you need, or is your next step to save a little money so you can get them?

Once you know if you have a goal (again, you don't have to) and name whatever your next step is, simply decide if you're ready to take it. You can say no, and it'll stay on The Someday List until you are.

How to Follow a Dream

Google tells me that a dream is "a cherished aspiration, ambition, or ideal,"* and I could not love that definition more. It's not just something you hope for, work toward, or believe in. It's something that's *cherished*. Dreams should be tenderly nurtured.

A trip is a dream. Learning a skill is a dream. But there are other kinds of dreams, ones that tend toward experiences, milestones, and maybe even some greatness.

Dreaming of greatness isn't bad. *It's just not where we start.* Greatness is not our primary objective or the carrot for our horse. That's why we're talking about this in chapter 18, not chapter 2.

The process to follow a dream is simple enough. Just treat your dream like anything else on The Someday List. Thought-

---

*Oxford Languages, to be exact. Sorry, Merriam-Webster.

fully consider when you're ready to do it, and then turn it into a project. It'll likely have *a lot* of steps and a distant end date because things that require aspiration, ambition, and idealism usually take some time. Nonetheless, you can still turn a dream into a project when you're ready.

But let's clear something up: You don't have to have big dreams.

The productivity industry loves big dreams, and there's not much wiggle room if you're not into them.

Dream big. BE big. Expand your impact.

And if you're not living that way, you probably just haven't found your big dream yet.

I vehemently disagree.

Your ordinary life has extraordinary value. You don't have to work to uncover a secret dream because there might not be one. Your dream also doesn't have to include hustle and influence and numbers. Dreams don't have to be measureable to have meaning.

> # Dreams don't have to be measureable to have meaning.

Everyone has the right to dream big, but that doesn't mean everyone has to.

It's all just life, and all of it counts.

TO RECAP

Enjoy the process of dreaming about trips, skills, and whatever you'd love to do someday. Follow the process to decide on your next trip or the questions to determine if you're ready to pursue a skill. And if you have a big dream, note that it gets broken down just like anything else. Whenever something is ready to become a project, re-read chapter 17.

Now go make your Someday List.

19. **Practice Checking In**

You've taken in a lot of information thus far.

Frameworks, numbered lists, acronyms, even daggum geometry.

Whenever I read a book with new ideas, I'm itching to get started, and I'm guessing that's true of you and your PLAN. You're starting with today and pursuing integration instead of greatness. You are befriending your menstrual cycle, bringing your whole self to the table, and making your Someday List. You can't wait to use The PLAN Pyramid, to Lighten the Load, and to plan your next week, month, season, or project.

You have that glow of inspiration.

I love that glow. I *live* for that glow. But that glow takes you only so far.

You need to pursue a *practice* of checking in with yourself and your PLAN if you want to experience its fullest benefits. Thankfully, The PLAN itself has a check-in movement already built in.

1. Prepare in the beginning.

2. Adjust in the middle.

3. Notice at the end.

This check-in practice will equip you to live based on what matters to you in the season you're in.

Let's practice checking in!

The Daily Check-In

In the morning, after naming what matters, consider what you need to prepare for today. What's on your palette? What's on your schedule? How can you prepare in a way that is kind and helpful to yourself?

You could prepare your to-do list, your office desk for a long day of work, your lunch so you have something to eat later, or your mental health with movement, meditation, music, or breath. There are no rules here. Every day is different, and what you need will be, too.

Around midday, consider what you need to adjust.

Adjust your energy, the tasks in front of you, and the expectations you have around them. Do you need to adjust what's for dinner, how much you can reasonably get done today, the tone of voice you're using with your kid? In light of where you are halfway through today, what could use an adjustment?

At the end of the day, notice how you're doing. How do you feel about your PLAN today? What do you notice in your body or in your home as you look around? What do you notice about the people you live with now that today is over? Take note of what's there.

If you want to use what you notice to influence tomorrow's preparation, you can take a moment to do that before you go to sleep.

The more you follow this rhythm and value those tiny check-in moments, the more grounded and whole you'll feel throughout the day.

The Weekly Check-In

We follow the same rhythm: Begin with what matters in your current season, then prepare in the beginning, adjust in the middle, and notice at the end.

At the start of the week, prepare for what's coming. Revisit chapter 14 if you want more direction on how to plan a week.

However, you *can* prepare too much too early, and when you do that, you're trying to control your life more than live it. Weekly preparation seems more helpful than daily preparation, but that's where they get you. The further you get from today, the fewer things there are to prepare because the fewer things *you know.* And the less you know, the more you scramble to control whatever you can. Big robot vibes, right there. Instead, remember that the more distant you are from a day, the less detailed your preparation needs to be.

Learning to pivot is better than learning to plan.

In the middle of a week, you do just that. You adjust.

I find the midweek check-in to be one of the best of all the check-ins. By Wednesday night, things I prepared on Monday are on the verge of being dusty and forgotten, and it's helpful to integrate adjustment into my rhythm. It's not settling or failing or something you call on in emergencies only. *Adjustment is part of the practice.*

Maybe what you started with on Monday had to change by Wednesday because of a broken water heater, a broken thumb, or even a broken heart. Don't power through. Instead, check in with yourself in the middle of the week and adjust your life to align with what matters.

At the end of the week, notice. Look back before you look forward. For many of us, those two happen in the same sitting, and they still can. Just make sure you don't skip ahead to preparing for the following week before noticing where you've been. Preparation is more effective when you incorporate the things you notice.

The Monthly Check-In

We still get to use the same rhythm: Prepare in the beginning, adjust in the middle, and notice at the end. However, the wider the range of time, the more attention you need to give to the bottom of your PLAN Pyramid, to what matters in this season of life.

Preparing for a new month is often more about mindset than about tasks. Tasks and tangible preparation are part of it, but if you go back to chapter 15, you'll see that when you plan a month, you paint with broader strokes: reflection, naming what matters, have-tos, and hope-tos. The monthly check-in is built into planning for the month, so if you do that, you're on your way.

In the middle of the month, check in and adjust. Let's say you do that at the end of the second week of the month. If you're in the rhythm of planning your week according to chapter 14, looking back on the previous week is already part of that process. All you need to do for your monthly check-in is look back a little further, to the beginning of the month, to see if your broader priorities for the month need adjusting. Whatever rhythm you're in, check in with yourself in the middle of each month.

At the end of the month, you look back and notice. How did things go? How are you feeling now that the month is over? How have you processed plans either working or not coming together at all? Just sit for a moment and look at where you've been.

Once again, how you plan any new month always begins with looking back, so noticing is integral to the process. If you have your own rhythm and process, that's awesome. I love it when people do what works for them. Just make sure noticing is part of your practice and look back on where you've been.

The Seasonal Check-In

Are you getting the hang of this now? Prepare in the beginning, adjust in the middle, and notice at the end.

I briefly mentioned the idea of opening and closing ceremonies in chapter 16, and this is the perfect time to talk about them in more detail.

> **An opening or closing seasonal ceremony is simply a tangible way to mark a moment in time.**

An opening or closing seasonal ceremony is simply a tangible way to mark a moment in time. It doesn't have to involve parties or processionals. You don't have to send out invitations, create something complicated, or even repeat the same thing year after year. A seasonal ceremony is just a way to prepare to enter a new season of life and celebrate where you are.

Let's say you're preparing for the summer, and after a busy, active spring, you decide that what matters this summer is having a ridiculous amount of fun. *Then open the summer with fun.* If your family already goes to the pool on the first day it opens, still do that, but make it matter. Give it just a hint of significance and make the experience of beginning The Summer of Fun sink deeper.

Every year, our family's fall opening ceremony is going to a local farm, walking the giant corn maze, taking a hayride, getting pumpkins, and going home and carving them despite the fact that kids usually abandon the process during the pumpkin clean-out. This is our most time-consuming seasonal ceremony because it usually takes half a day, but it's a memorable half a day that marks the beginning of a season we love. Yours can take hours, minutes, or a moment.

In your own way, prepare for your season by having an opening ceremony.

When it's time to adjust in the middle of a season, you might not feel like there's much to do. If you're already checking in daily, weekly, and monthly or even just keeping The PLAN Pyramid in mind, adjustment is on your radar. You're learning that pivoting is not a cop-out but a natural part of how to live well. Well done.

But sometimes we need a tiny burst of life in the middle of a season, particularly a weary one. Is there a way to mark that midseason moment? Can you take a fun outing, see friends you haven't hung out with in a while, or just have a chill day where everybody stays at home and does a beautiful dose of nothing? If you know the middle, mark the middle. *We're here! We're doing it!* A little midseason ceremony is a great way to do that.

Finally, when you come to the end of a season, notice where you are. Notice who you've become. Notice what you released and what you embraced. Notice how you're feeling about yourself and what you've learned about your ability to live through another season.

And if you're feeling sparkly, have a closing ceremony.

Give this past season its time in the light. Raise a glass. Throw a party. Burn old schoolwork in a fire. Ring the bell at the cancer treatment center for the last time and then celebrate.

You did it. You made it.

Notice it.

The Heartbeat Check-In

All of these check-ins are connected to time, but what about when you need a check-in right now?

Try the Heartbeat Check-In.

When you're feeling overwhelmed, tired, unsettled, or untethered, follow the same movements, just way more quickly and in your body instead of in your planner. This is almost like a breath prayer or mantra, something you say as you breathe in and out. Regardless of the label, here's what you do.

Prepare by grounding your body. Maybe put your hand on your heart, hold your own hands, close your eyes, or sit outside on the grass. Whatever you do, just be still a second.

Next, adjust your body and mind as you breathe in, and then notice what happens as you breathe out. If you want, you can even use some of the phrases from earlier chapters as you do.

Breathe in: *Now isn't forever.*

Breathe out: *Good is here right now.*

Breathe in: *Now isn't forever.*

Breathe out: *Good is here right now.*

Doing this Heartbeat Check-In takes seconds. It's just closing your eyes and breathing on purpose, maybe with a few words if you want, but it sure does make a difference.

Prepare your body, adjust as you breathe in, and notice as you breathe out. As you do, wholeness grows, and you live as your truest self, no matter what is happening around you.

TO RECAP

Regardless of when, how, or why you do a check-in, the rhythm stays the same: Prepare in the beginning, adjust in the middle, notice at the end.

This book is full of ideas, but reading them isn't enough. If you want to really *live,* learn to check in.

Checklists are fun. Check-ins are better.

20. When You're Done Reading This Book

Your time is precious, and I'm honored you've spent some of it reading *The PLAN*.

When I get to the end of a book like this, I want to flip a switch and apply everything at once. I feel light and inspired and ready to take on the world.

But that's the old paradigm talking. Remember, you have a new goal. It's not greatness. It's not an imagined future. It's not optimization or efficiency or taking on the world.

Your new goal is to live an integrated life that starts exactly where you are.

Start small with today. Rest on what matters in this season of life. Don't attempt to prepare your life according to everything in this book because you'll only get a lopsided pyramid. Instead, begin the daily practice of preparing, adjusting, and noticing in equal measure so you can live a life that matters to you.

When you're ready to try a new strategy or you need a reminder of a particular principle, revisit the chapter and read it through the lens of where you are now. If you want to quickly reference something, remember the Quick-Reference Guide in the back. It'll have all the mindsets, principles, and basics of The PLAN in one place so you can access what you need when you need it.

I hope you will come back to this book again and again as your seasons change and will stay kind to yourself as they do.

It's been my absolute pleasure to write this book for you, and I hope it has met you exactly where you are. And no matter where that is, remember that good is here right now.

Deep breath.

Let's live *today*.

Part Three

Pep Talks

No matter how thoughtful, intentional, or calm you try to be, some days just feel like garbage.

When you find yourself wanting to hide, panic, rage, or start over, read one of these pep talks instead. While they are not intended to be quick fixes, they might help you catch your breath long enough to prevent you from throwing away all your children's toys, buying seven new planners, or rage-looking for a new job.

When you need to remember what matters, these pep talks are ready and waiting.

21. **When There's Too Much to Do**

If you just opened your planner and then fell into a heap on the floor, you're in the right place. I'm quite familiar with the scheduling fetal position.

First, take a deep breath. You're not in danger, logistically or otherwise. You're an amazing person, and you're going to be okay. Breathe.

Next, let me shoot you straight: The reason you think there's too much to do is that *there probably is,* and now you do have to do something about it. However, do not, under any circumstances, start turning yourself into a logistical pretzel so you can figure out how to do all of this on your own. That is the wrong answer.

Instead, you have to let something go.

I know you hate hearing that and want to punch me in the boob for even saying it. Still, I'll risk the bruise since I know I'm right on this one. You cannot tend to or complete everything on your list. You're an incredibly capable person, so if you're feeling overwhelmed, *that means you are.*

When there's too much to do, it's because everything feels like it has to happen *now,* making this a great time to look at your life through the lens of urgency. Remember the Now, Soon, Later, Never Mind list? Try that here. Identify what really needs to be done now and leave the rest for a little further down the road.

You might say, "Kendra, I can't! All of this is important!" But I call BS because you have already let something important go, and it's most likely yourself. In your pursuit of doing all there is to do, are you sleeping? Have you hung out with a friend recently? When was the last time you had fun? My guess is that even if you've checked off your list, *you've checked out on yourself.*

I don't want you to do that anymore. You're lovely and deserve to live your life in a whole, integrated way, and we both know that running yourself ragged is not the way to do that. If you're already willing to say no to yourself, learn to be willing to say no to something less important than *you.*

Breathe deeply, apply some reasonable urgency to what's in front of you, let some of it go, and compassionately accept that not everything can matter right now. You've got this.

22. **When Your Plan Falls Apart**

Disappointment is the worst. You worked so hard to put this plan together, and you thought it would work. Then something out of your control knocked your plan off course, and now you feel like a dirty sandwich bag dangerously close to a tornado of big feelings.

Don't try to talk yourself out of how you feel. It's okay to be bummed. Just be bummed in a kind way.

Remember, plans are just intentions, not pass-fail. Your plan didn't work, but that doesn't mean anything is wrong with *you*. You're not a failure, you're not an idiot, and you're not missing anything that "everyone else" has. You just had a plan that didn't work. It happens all the time.

And since it happens all the time, get comfortable with learning to pivot. Remember, learning to pivot is more important than learning to plan. Instead of beating yourself up for not getting something right, embrace your ability to notice and adjust when a plan goes off script. You *can* pivot. You can learn that skill and get better at it over time and even become fulfilled by it. Revisit chapter 11 if you need a refresher.

If you feel like your plans keep falling apart because of their actual construction, you are reading the right book to help you correct your form. It could be that you're planning with a skewed view of preparation (chapter 5) or according to the goals of the productivity industry (chapter 2). We're doing something different, something that might need revisiting from time to time.

The truth is, failed plans don't feel good, but that doesn't mean *you* are not good. Ultimately, be kind to yourself. Celebrate your ability to pivot.

23. **When You Can't Say No**

Did you just volunteer to bring cupcakes to the class party to-morrow even though you have no ingredients in the house for dinner, let alone for cupcakes? Did you tell your kid that they could do both cross-country and drama club this semester even though you do not have enough adults, vehicles, or time machines to make that happen? Did you assume the responsibility to plan your annual girls' trip even though you're swamped with work and adrenal fatigue?

A lot of folks, especially women, struggle to say no, so you're not alone. However, it's not a bad idea to start trying.

My guess is that you say yes because the person asking for help matters to you—your friend, your kid, your boss, your mom, your neighbor. Your yes to their request is a yes to *them,* and that is a beautiful thing. The world is a better place because of people like you who care about others.

However, letting everyone else dictate how you spend your time is not sustainable. It might even lead to resentment, and we don't want that.

Instead, try these three tips.

First, decide once on a no. Case-by-case yeses require too much energy, so remove that load where you can by deciding to say no to a certain kind of request once and for all (in this season). Say no to hosting anything at your house for the next month, to taking on any new clients, to attending evening meetings, to trying new recipes, or to volunteering at your kid's school. It doesn't matter what it is. Just decide once on a no that would help lighten the load in this season. Now isn't forever.

Second, separate the task from the person. You are not saying no to the person; you are saying no to the task. You can still communicate how much you value someone without saying yes to everything they ask of you. Similarly, separate the task from *yourself*. Just because you say no doesn't mean you're a bad person, mother, daughter, or friend. You can exist in that relationship without carrying all its weight.

Third, remember that you can't be everything to everyone. *Even if you think you're pulling it off,* you're not. You will find yourself lying on the floor, slowly moaning because you can't keep up. My goal is to keep you from floor moaning, but you will always end up there if you ignore this concept.

You cannot be everything to everyone. Sip that slowly like an expensive bourbon. It's not even bad news, pal. It's *freedom*. Plus, if you have kids, especially if you have daughters, show them that healthy, loving, deep relationships are possible without saying yes to everything.

Start small in saying no, but please just *start*. You can do this.

24. **When You Feel Guilty**

Guilt does not play fair.

You might feel guilty because you messed up. You missed a friend's birthday, forgot to get a kid from practice, or haven't called your dad in so long that now it feels weird to do it at all.

You might feel guilty because you're not doing enough. You don't cook homemade dinners, you don't have enough energy to keep up with current events, or you are forty-three years old and still trying to figure out a laundry rhythm.

You might even feel guilty because you are doing something for yourself. You spend money to take a fun trip, you let the dirty dishes wait in the sink while you read, or you let your partner clean up the living room without getting up to help.

You feel guilty when you do too much, too little, or just enough. It's not fair, but it's also to be expected. Remember, women are held to higher standards of productivity without the tools to meet them or the power to change them. We feel guilty because we keep losing at a game we were never meant to play and, frankly, shouldn't even want to win.

So, when you feel guilty, remember that you live by a different paradigm.

The goal is not greatness; it's integration.

You're not trying to do everything, be everything, and judge every day against the "best" day. Instead, you are seeking wholeness within yourself even when circumstances feel off, expectations go unmet, feelings get hurt, or your needs take center stage.

Guilt itself implies an offense or a wrongdoing, and most of the time, what you're feeling guilty about is not wrong. And even when it is, when you do hurt someone or mess up, you can mend what is broken. In fact, relationships become stronger *because of* repair.

So, rather than sitting in the guilt or hustling to avoid it, tell yourself the truth. Have you done anything wrong? If not, release the guilt. It's not yours to carry. If you did do something wrong, move toward the beauty and health of repair.

You're just a person trying to live a meaningful life. Don't let unnecessary guilt rob you of that.

25. When You Don't Have Help

Listen to me right now. Living life alone is impossible. Unequivocally, decidedly impossible.

So, if you have to do it, you definitely feel it.

You might be single and are therefore the only grown-up in your home who makes all the decisions. This is exhausting. You might have an unhelpful partner and live with an uneven division of labor or an unequal amount of rest. That kind of disparity will wreak havoc on a relationship, and havoc is not recommended. You might not have the financial resources to afford the help you need, things like a house cleaner, convenience foods, or regular childcare. That requires you to either do something yourself or leave it undone.

When you don't have help, you also don't have hope, and that can bleed a person dry.

If you are in a situation where there are literally no people or resources to help you out, take a small step toward seeking some. Join a mom group. Offer freelance services to a handful of people in your circle and make some extra money to hire a house cleaner. Find potential community in a civic organization, church, or professional group. Tell a faraway friend or family member that you're lonely and ask if y'all can talk on the phone one evening a week for some companionship while you find your way in a new place. Don't assume there is no help for anything ever. Start small and look for help.

I've seen people on the internet comment on how ridiculous and fruitless it is to ask for help, especially in the areas of childcare and domestic life. "Who am I supposed to ask to help me? My friends? My neighbors? Who are these people? And what am I supposed to ask them? Are they going to clean my disgusting toilet? Are they going to drive my carpool or figure out how to deal with the bat problem in my attic? Are they going to come over and sit with my screaming kid?" Maybe not. But those aren't the only things on your plate.

Can a friend pick up a rotisserie chicken for your dinner? Yep.

Can your neighbor hang out in the yard with your other kid who isn't screaming? Yep.

Can your sister sit with you in your house or on FaceTime while you fold the seventeenth load of laundry that day? Yep.

Can you text a friend group about how hard today has been and receive some solidarity? Yep.

Don't assume that because you can't get help for everything, there is no help for anything.

26. **When You're Not Motivated**

According to the dictionary, motivation is "the general desire or willingness of someone to do something."[1]

If you do not have the desire or willingness to do something, maybe that thing matters less than you thought. Feel free to let it go.

If you do not have the desire or willingness to do something that *does* matter, consider a reframe.

- Laundry isn't an endless chore trying to suffocate you. It's refilling drawers and closets with clothes that make you and your people feel like themselves. Or it keeps everyone from being naked. Take your pick.

- Tidying isn't cleaning up everybody's mess. It's creating space for living life.

- Exercise isn't about getting smaller. It's a liturgy of movement that tends to your body.

- Cooking dinner isn't another thankless time suck. It's a way to love yourself and your people no matter how ungrateful they are for the nourishment.

If you *do* have the desire and willingness to do something but can't seem to, the problem isn't motivation. It's task initiation.

Task initiation is an executive functioning skill that's all about "getting going," and it might be hard to access depending on your brain chemistry or the burden of your circumstances.

Don't say you're not motivated when you're just struggling to get started. Those are two different things, so label your situation kindly and correctly, please.

If you can't initiate a task, start as small as humanly possible, as small as just standing up. If you can't even do that, give yourself a countdown in your head: *On three, I'm going to stand up.* Count, and then stand. You are initiating the task. If that's as far as you get, that's okay. Sometimes movement is significantly challenging, and you're still a lovely person.

If standing helps, do the next smallest thing. Walk to the sink. Pick up the paper. Turn on the dryer. Once you have initiated the task, don't expect yourself to do the entire thing, especially if it's large. You're not trying to complete the task, just get it going. If you keep it going, awesome. If you don't, also awesome.

Start where you are and be kind to yourself no matter where that is.

27. **When You're Just So Tired**

If you're tired, go to sleep.

Like, for real. Go take a nap. I particularly love the Seventeen-Minute Nap.

Put on some white noise because sometimes other humans are around, set a timer for seventeen minutes, and close your eyes. If you sleep, great. If you don't, also great. When you feel tired, stillness is valuable even if you don't sleep.

Seventeen minutes is a great amount for me (and has anecdotally been validated by many others) because it's enough to get me refreshed but not so much that I wake up groggy and more tired than when I started.

If you do not have access to a soft space and an empty seventeen minutes, you still need rest.

Consistently feeling tired means you probably need a consistent approach, so here are a few things to consider.

One, are you doing too much during the day? Are you listening to what your body is telling you? Are you paying attention to your hormones and managing your energy as intentionally as you can? Sleep isn't always the answer, so notice if how you're living day to day is contributing to your tiredness.

Two, is your sleep restorative? Maybe the hours are fine, but the sleep itself is not. Some people swear by sleep gummies. Others use sleep apps that monitor REM cycles and wake you up in the morning during a window of light sleep so you feel refreshed. Notice if the sleep itself needs a little attention.

Three, are you going to bed late? I know you probably have a lot happening during the day, with little time to do anything for yourself. Instead of heading to bed early every single night, do it sometimes. You don't have to have a fixed bedtime. Enjoy those late nights alongside the longer sleeps. I think both matter.

Finally, are you waiting for a magical vacation or long stretch of rest to get back on track? That's not a thing. Rest is required every single day, and letting your tiredness accumulate only makes matters worse. You've seen it floating around the internet plenty of times, but I'll say it here, too: Rest is not a reward. It's a right. A requirement. Please stop waiting to rest until you have more time to do it. You probably won't. You haven't yet, so who are we kidding?

Rest, please. Do it every day in whatever way makes the most sense for you.

28. When You Wish Things Were Different

Some days, the life you have isn't the life you want.

It might be a big thing like not being married, being married to someone you don't always like, having a job that isn't what you expected, living in a place you don't love but not having the money or ability to move, watching someone you love go through a terrible season and being powerless to change it, being in a stage of life that you don't like and still having a pretty long way to go before you're out of it.

That is a hard place to be, friend.

You might also wish something small but distracting was different: your haircut, your kid's attitude toward homework, your desk being so far from a window.

Everyone at some point wishes things were different, and here are three reminders for when that happens to you.

One, you're allowed to care.

If you want something to change, it means you care about something that's missing. That is allowed, and that is good. Caring doesn't make you selfish; it makes you human.

Two, good is here right now.

When you wish things were different, you tend to focus on the discouraging parts of your season or situation. Be honest about where you are, but also remember that good is here right now. No matter what's going on, good exists. Even if it's just the kindness and goodness that exist in you, there is good here right now.

Three, try a Heartbeat Check-In.

Turn to chapter 19 for a reminder, but essentially you breathe in and out, ground yourself where you are, perhaps with some helpful phrases, and be kind to yourself as you remain there.

Hard seasons are no joke, and it's okay to wish they were different. Don't ignore your struggles or push them away. You can also access kindness toward yourself and notice the good that's around you. You can simultaneously be present with your challenges and notice the good they bring. Remember, two things can be true at once.

29. When You Don't Have a Plan

I want to talk to the planners first.

A plan is helpful, but it is not a requirement. If you go into a situation without a plan, you will not explode. Your humanity will not catch fire. Your soul will not crumble under the weight of spontaneity. It's all going to be okay.

If you are *not* a planner, a plan is helpful but still not a requirement. You are not a child. You are not incompetent. You should embrace your natural ability to pivot and not be embarrassed by it.

Those are the broad strokes. Now to the practicality.

Let's say you don't have a plan but need one. Something has sprung up, and it's time to think ahead and figure out a possible path. This applies to an annoying leak in the ceiling all the way to an impromptu invitation to somebody's lake house. All sorts of things need a plan.

If you don't have a plan, start where you are. Put a bucket under the leak. Say yes to the lake house. Notice your energy, resources, and circumstances, and tend to what you need right now. Don't turn yourself into a robot, even for something great. Just be a person and start where you are with what you have.

Next, name what matters. A plan is a series of possible decisions, and when we don't know what's most important, decisions make us oh so tired. Name what matters about what you're doing *before* you make a plan.

If you're a natural planner, you can carry on perfectly well from here. You have your own beautiful ways of doing things, and I wish you well in whatever you're doing.

If you're not a natural planner, or if you just don't have the energy to think right now, turn to the chapter that best fits the type of plan you're trying to make.

In all of it, start small right where you are. Plans are the most helpful one decision at a time.

Quick-Reference Guide

Two Beliefs That Will Change Everything

- The goal is not greatness. The goal is **integration.**

- Don't start from the future. **Start where you are.**

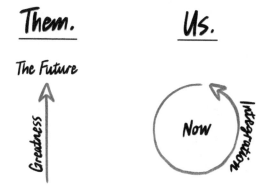

Naming What Matters

- **Proactively** name what matters by making what matters **singular** and then making it **smaller.**

- **Reactively** name what matters by either **trusting your gut** or **trusting the priority you already named.**

The PLAN Pyramid

- The base is **what matters right now in your current season.**

- The three sides are **prepare, adjust,** and **notice.**

  - To **prepare,** go in the right order.

  - To **adjust,** start small.

  - To **notice,** be kind to yourself.

- The apex is **live.**

  - To **live,** live in the season.

PLAN Mindsets

Prepare—go in the right order

1. Not everything can matter.

2. A plan is an intention, not pass-fail.

3. External solutions will not solve internal problems.

Live—live in the season

1. Do not judge every day against your best day.

2. Contentment is the antidote to optimization.

3. You're allowed to care.

Adjust—start small

1. Match your expectations to the energy you're willing to give.

2. Now isn't forever.

3. You're allowed to change your mind.

Notice—be kind to yourself

1. Staying grounded is better than staying on task.

2. Your body is wise.

3. Good is here right now.

The Menstrual Cycle

- Menstrual Phase/Winter—Notice (approx. days 1 to 5)

- Follicular Phase/Spring—Prepare (approx. days 6 to 12)

- Ovulation Phase/Summer—Live (approx. days 13 to 18)

- Luteal Phase/Fall—Adjust (approx. day 19 until your period starts)

Manage the Right Thing

- Notice your energy.

- Adjust your expectations.

- Prepare to pivot.

    1. Breathe.

    2. Actively seek softness.

    3. Name what matters.

    4. Make the problem smaller.

    5. Solve the problem.

- Live together.

The TODAY Framework

For an energetic *today:*

- **T**ricky

- **O**ptional

- **D**elightful

- **A**ctive

- **Y**es

For a gentle *today:*

- **T**ender

- **O**utput

- **D**elegate

- **A**ccept

- **Y**es

The Lighten the Load Framework

1. Make It Visible *(get it out so you can figure it out)*

2. Make It Matter *(assign significance to everything)*

3. Make It Smaller *(turn projects and chaos into decisions and actions)*

4. Make It Happen *(put everything in its place)*

    *   Now, Soon, Later, Never Mind is organized by **urgency.**

    *   What's in the Tank is organized by **energy.**

    *   All Together Now is organized by **similarity.**

    *   Pick One is chosen with **humanity.**

The Lazy Genius Method

1. Prioritize—name what matters

2. Essentialize—have what you need and get rid of what's in the way

3. Organize—put everything in its place

4. Personalize—feel like yourself

5. Systemize—stay in the flow

Thirteen Lazy Genius Principles

1. Decide Once

2. Start Small

3. Ask the Magic Question

4. Live in the Season

5. Build the Right Routines

6. Set House Rules

7. Put Everything in Its Place

8. Let People In

9. Batch It

10. Essentialize

11. Go in the Right Order

12. Schedule Rest

13. Be Kind to Yourself

Acknowledgments

To the team at Convergent: It means the world that you brought your energy and expertise so enthusiastically to this project. Tina Constable and Campbell Wharton, thank you for fighting for me.

To my editor, Susan Tjaden, and my agent, Lisa Jackson: You both have been with me since the beginning, and I couldn't be in better hands. Thank you.

To the greatest team ever assembled in all the internet world: Leslie Fox, Leah Jarvis, and Letoya Monteith, I literally could not do any of this without you, nor would I want to.

To Allison Smoak: You started praying for me when I was not only in the thick of writing this book but going through more personal heartbreak than I had the capacity for. I don't even know how to say thank you. Your faithfulness to me, someone who was really a stranger, was deeply sacred, and there aren't words to describe how grateful I am.

To my friends, both internet and IRL: It makes my heart hurt when I think about how good I have it. There are too many of you to name, and that alone is an embarrassment of riches. Thank you, friends, for being my friend.

To Erin Moon: I thought of you the whole time. Love you mean it.

To Nora McInerny: I'm not sure this would've happened without our phone call. Honestly, thank you.

To Jamie Golden, Bri McKoy, and Laura Tremaine: You walked with me through this book like you walk with me through all my work, and I'll never get over it. You're the best colleagues that have (lol, begrudgingly) become friends. Love you forever.

To Emily P. Freeman: What would I do without you? Who would I be?! Where would I go?! It's all too much to think about. You've heard more of my ramblings than anybody, save my actual husband, and I'm excessively glad you're my person.

To Han: I won the sister lottery hands down and love you so much. When my life is chaotic, thank you for being a safe place to land.

To Mom: You're a huge reason why this book is in people's hands. Thank you for doing the practical things like getting the kids from school, running my errands, and putting the new groceries behind the old ones without my having to ask you to. I'm also really glad that this book came to life the same time that you did. The two aren't related, but it's fun to think about it anyway. I love who you are, and I'm proud of how hard you've fought for her. Thank you for being such a wonderful mom.

To my squeezable, precious, giant children: Being your mom is the most special thing of all the things, and I'll never stop telling you I love you, even though you say you already know.

To Kaz: You're almost annoyingly supportive. I keep waiting for you to not ask how you can help, to not want to celebrate something small, or to be frustrated that I'm going to hole up in another Airbnb to write *again,* and yet here we are. You're still gladly helping and celebrating in every way possible. Thank you for rubbing my back, listening to me ramble, and tidying up before I get home because you know that matters to me. This work would not be the same without you, and neither would I. You're the best person of all the persons, and I love you like crazy.

To the Lazy Genius community: I hope this book meets you exactly where you are. Thank you for being the reason I love my job.

In all things, thanks be to God.

Notes

Chapter 1: The Real Reason Planning Is Hard

1. *Sabrina,* directed by Sydney Pollack, screenplay by Barbara Benedek and David Rayfiel (Los Angeles, Calif.: Paramount Pictures, 1995).
2. Abby McCain, "20+ Trending U.S. Wedding Industry Statistics [2023]: How Big Is the Wedding Industry," Zippia, March 14, 2023, www.zippia.com/advice/wedding-industry-statistics.
3. "Correctional Facilities in the US—Market Size, Industry Analysis, Trends and Forecasts (2024–2029)," IBISWorld, March 2023, www.ibisworld.com/united-states/market-research-reports/correctional-facilities-industry/.
4. "Productivity Software—Worldwide," Statista, March 2023, www.statista.com/outlook/tmo/software/productivity-software/worldwide.

Chapter 2: Two Beliefs That Will Change Everything

1. Brené Brown, "Ten Guideposts for Wholehearted Living," https://brenebrown.com/art/ten-guideposts-for-wholehearted-living-3.
2. Aundi Kolber, *Strong Like Water: Finding the Freedom, Safety, and Compassion to Move Through Hard Things—and Experience True Flourishing* (Carol Stream, Ill.: Tyndale, 2023), 216.
3. Kolber, *Strong Like Water,* 217.
4. Lewis Howes, *The School of Greatness: A Real-World Guide to Living Bigger, Loving Deeper, and Leaving a Legacy* (New York: Rodale, 2015), xvii–xviii.

Chapter 4: Here's The PLAN

1. Oliver Burkeman, *Four Thousand Weeks: Time Management for Mortals* (New York: Farrar, Straus and Giroux, 2021), 67.

2. Stacy A. Cordery, *Alice: Alice Roosevelt Longworth, from White House Princess to Washington Power Broker* (New York: Penguin, 2007), 465.

Chapter 5: How to Prepare

1. Oliver Burkeman, *Four Thousand Weeks: Time Management for Mortals* (New York: Farrar, Straus and Giroux, 2021), 62.
2. Emily Field, Alexis Krivkovich, Sandra Kügele, Nicole Robinson, and Lareina Yee, "Women in the Workplace 2023," McKinsey & Company, October 5, 2023, www.mckinsey.com/featured-insights/diversity-and -inclusion/women-in-the-workplace.

Chapter 6: How to Live

1. Julia Manini and Anne-Joyelle Occhicone, *The Great Pause: Persever-ance Through the Pandemic* (Manitoba: FriesenPress, 2022), 4.

Chapter 8: How to Notice

1. Hillary L. McBride, *The Wisdom of Your Body: Finding Healing, Wholeness, and Connection Through Embodied Living* (Grand Rapids, Mich.: Brazos Press, 2021), 6.

Chapter 9: Let's Talk About Periods

1. Cecilia Tasca, Mariangela Rapetti, Mauro Giovanni Carta, and Bianca Fadda, "Women and Hysteria in the History of Mental Health," *Clinical Practice and Epidemiology in Mental Health* 8 (2012), https://ncbi .nlm.nih.gov/pmc/articles/PMC3480686.
2. Tasca, Rapetti, Carta, and Fadda, "Women and Hysteria."
3. Tasca, Rapetti, Carta, and Fadda, "Women and Hysteria."
4. Kate Northrup, *Do Less: A Revolutionary Approach to Time and Energy Management for Busy Moms* (Carlsbad, Calif.: Hay House, 2019), 135.
5. Maisie Hill, *Period Power: Harness Your Hormones and Get Your Cycle Working for You* (London: Green Tree, 2019), 63.
6. "How the Pill Works," PBS, www.pbs.org/wgbh/americanexperience /features/pill-how-pill-works.
7. Heidi Ledford, "How Menopause Reshapes the Brain," *Nature,* May 3, 2023, www.nature.com/articles/d41586-023-01474-3.

Chapter 10: Bring Your Whole Self to the Table

1. KC Davis, *How to Keep House While Drowning: A Gentle Approach to Cleaning and Organizing* (New York: Simon and Schuster, 2022), 6.
2. Elizabeth Grace Saunders, "A Way to Plan If You're Bad at Planning,"

Harvard Business Review, July 4, 2017, https://hbr.org/2017/07
/a-way-to-plan-if-youre-bad-at-planning.

3. "Attention-Deficit/Hyperactivity Disorder," National Institute of
Mental Health, www.nimh.nih.gov/health/statistics/attention-deficit
-hyperactivity-disorder-adhd.

4. Dan Witters, "U.S. Depression Rates Reach New Highs," Gallup,
May 17, 2023, https://news.gallup.com/poll/505745/depression
-rates-reach-new-highs.aspx.

5. "Depressive Disorder (Depression)," World Health Organization,
March 31, 2023, www.who.int/news-room/fact-sheets/detail
/depression.

6. Luke 12:25 in The Holy Bible, New International Version®, NIV®.
Copyright © 1973, 1978, 1984, 2011 by Biblica Inc.™

Chapter 11: Manage the Right Thing

1. Oliver Burkeman, *Four Thousand Weeks: Time Management for
Mortals* (New York: Farrar, Straus and Giroux, 2021), 187.

2. Robert Waldinger and Marc Schulz, *The Good Life: Lessons from the
World's Longest Scientific Study of Happiness* (New York: Simon &
Schuster, 2023).

3. Robert D. Putnam, *Bowling Alone: The Collapse and Revival of
American Community* (New York: Simon & Schuster, 2001).

4. *Lost,* season 1, episode 5, "White Rabbit," written by Jeffrey Lieber,
J. J. Abrams, and Damon Lindelof, directed by Kevin Hooks, aired
October 20, 2004, on ABC.

Chapter 12: Start with Today

1. Wendy Molyneux (@wendymolyneux), Twitter, https://twitter.com
/sstoneb/status/1494618823936430081?lang=en.

2. Paraphrased Joyce Chong, "5 Reasons Why Modern Life Causes Us
Stress (and What to Do About It)," Skill Collective, July 2023, https://
theskillcollective.com/blog/modern-life-causes-stress.

3. Celeste Headlee, *Do Nothing: How to Break Away from Overworking,
Overdoing, and Underliving* (New York: Harmony, 2020), 93.

4. "Multitasking: Switching Costs," American Psychological Association,
March 20, 2006, www.apa.org/topics/research/multitasking.

5. "America's #1 Health Problem," American Institute of Stress, www
.stress.org/americas-1-health-problem.

Chapter 13: How to Make a Better To-Do List

1. Robert N. Kraft, "10 Benefits of Making Lists," *Psychology Today,*
May 7, 2021, www.psychologytoday.com/us/blog/defining-memories
/202105/10-benefits-making-lists.

2. Celeste Headlee, *Do Nothing: How to Break Away from Overworking, Overdoing, and Underliving* (New York: Harmony, 2020), 89.
3. *Merriam-Webster,* s.v. "brain dump," www.merriam-webster.com /dictionary/brain%20dump.
4. Charles Darwin, letter to Susan Darwin (sister), Bahia, Brazil, August 4, 1836.

Chapter 14: Plan a Week

1. *Merriam-Webster,* s.v. "bunting," www.merriam-webster.com /dictionary/bunting.

Chapter 15: Plan a Month

1. Emily P. Freeman, "10 Questions for Reflection & Discernment," https://emilypfreeman.com/10questions.

Chapter 17: Plan a Project

1. Chris Pavone, *Two Nights in Lisbon* (New York: Farrar, Straus and Giroux, 2022), 136.

Chapter 26: When You're Not Motivated

1. *Oxford English Dictionary,* s.v. "motivation," www.oed.com/dictionary /motivation_n?tab=factsheet#35683504.

About the Author

Kendra Adachi is the two-time *New York Times* bestselling author of *The Lazy Genius Way* and *The Lazy Genius Kitchen* and host of the nationally ranked *The Lazy Genius Podcast.* As an expert in compassionate time management, Kendra helps others stop doing it all for the sake of doing what matters. She lives in North Carolina with her husband and three kids.

ALSO AVAILABLE FROM
KENDRA ADACHI